MENTAL HEALTH AND JEDIISM PHILOSOPHY

By
Richard R.Dudley

Table of Contents

Chapter 1: Introduction of Jedi Philosophy

In the vast tapestry of narratives woven throughout the *Star Wars* saga, one thread consistently emerges as a source of guidance, hope, and resilience: the philosophy of the Jedi. This ancient yet ever-relevant wisdom speaks to the core of what it means to navigate the complexities of existence whether in the vastness of a galaxy far, far away or within the confines of a prison.

As we embark on this exploration of Jedi philosophy, we will uncover the fundamental principles that resonate with the struggles of those who find themselves behind bars, offering a pathway toward emotional resilience and personal transformation.

At the heart of Jedi philosophy lies the concept of balance. The Force, as described within the lore, is a mystical energy that binds all living things. It encompasses both light and dark, good and bad, and operates on the principle that harmony is necessary for a healthy existence. For inmates grappling with their own internal battles, understanding this duality is critical. Just as the Force is composed of opposing elements, so too are the emotions and experiences that shape human lives. Anger, sadness, fear, and joy coexist within us, and recognizing this balance can serve as a powerful first step toward emotional clarity and healing.

The Jedi teachings encourage practitioners to be mindful of their thoughts and feelings, emphasizing the importance of living in the moment. Mindfulness a practice that has gained momentum in modern psychology finds its echo in the teachings of the Jedi. By focusing on the present, individuals can better manage the turmoil that often accompanies past regrets or future anxieties. In a prison environment, where time can feel stagnant yet filled with relentless pressure, cultivating mindfulness through Jedi practices can provide inmates with a means to escape the confines of their own minds, if only temporarily.

This idea of inner peace is a recurring theme within Jedi philosophy. The journey of a Jedi is not simply one of external prowess mastery of lightsabers or physical combat but also an inner quest for tranquility and understanding. Jedi are trained to confront their fears, to face their doubts, and to emerge not just unscathed but more enlightened. Imagine an inmate, once consumed by the chaos of their own thoughts, finding solace through a conscious effort to channel their inner Jedi, gracefully navigating the complexities of their experiences and emerging with newfound strength.

Several anecdotes from the vast lore of the Jedi illustrate these concepts. Take, for instance, the story of Yoda, one of the most revered Jedi Masters. He spent years in exile, a period marked not only by physical separation from the galaxy's turmoil but also by a personal journey to understand the nature of the Force, the interplay of light and dark, and his own shortcomings. Yoda's wisdom involved recognizing failure as a vital part of growth. This narrative emphasizes the importance of embracing one's past while remaining focused on the future a lesson that holds immense value for inmates searching for personal redemption.

Additionally, the training of Anakin Skywalker serves as a cautionary tale steeped in Jedi teachings. Anakin's rise and fall illustrate the peril of imbalance and how unchecked emotions can lead to destruction rather than healing. His tragic story is a reminder that the struggle for balance within oneself is a continuous journey one that requires vigilance, humility, and a supportive community. For inmates, this narrative can inspire critical reflection. It encourages them to consider their desires, fears, and motivations, ultimately urging them to seek a path that fosters growth, connection, and understanding rather than isolation and despair.

The relevance of these ancient teachings in contemporary struggles cannot be overstated. For those living within the walls of a correctional facility, the challenges are multifaceted ranging from the stress of confinement to the difficulties of re-entering society after serving time. In such an environment, where emotional turmoil is common, the principles of Jedi philosophy resonate deeply. The call to find balance, maintain mindfulness, and seek inner peace offers a counter-narrative to external chaos.

Institutions and programs that seek to assist inmates can draw from these fundamental principles, integrating them into rehabilitative approaches. Group discussions centered on Jedi philosophy can foster a sense of belonging and collective healing. When inmates engage in these teachings together, they share their insights and experiences, creating a community grounded in support, understanding, and shared growth. By reframing their perspectives through the lens of the Jedi both individually and collectively inmates can find a renewed sense of purpose in their journeys.

Practical applications of Jedi wisdom extend into the daily activities of prison life. Simple practices such as meditation, breathwork, or reflective journaling aligned with Jedi teachings can empower inmates to reclaim their narratives. These practices teach them to step back, observe their thoughts without judgment, and make conscious choices about how to respond to their emotions rather than reacting impulsively. The process of reclaiming agency over one's responses is a profound act of resilience, and it aligns seamlessly with the journey of a Jedi.

Furthermore, creating opportunities for inmates to explore their own identities through the framework of Jedi philosophy can be transformative. Self-reflection, interspersed with the rich lore of the Jedi, helps individuals examine their life stories. Each inmate becomes the hero of a narrative shaped not by their past mistakes but by their aspirations for redemption. It empowers them to recognize that though they may have lost their way, their journey does not end in darkness. Rather, it presents an opportunity to gain experience, to change, and to rise in the light.

As we conclude this exploration of Jedi philosophy, it becomes clear that these ancient teachings hold extraordinary relevance for anyone seeking to navigate their inner world amidst external chaos. Whether faced with the confines of a physical prison or the emotional prisons we construct for ourselves, the journey of the Jedi offers hope. It beckons individuals to embrace the Force within, to cultivate balance, and to strive for mindfulness and inner peace.

The lessons found within this philosophy not only uplift those struggling in their present circumstances but also provide a framework for contemplating future possibilities a future that shines with the light of transformation, resilience, and redemption. Let this introduction serve as an invitation to dive deeper into the symbiosis of Jedi wisdom and modern rehabilitative practices an invitation to rise, even in the face of adversity, and embody the spirit of the Force. As we move forward, we will explore practical applications, stories of transformation, and the ongoing journey toward harmony that awaits within these ancient yet timeless philosophical teachings.

Jedi Traits: Courage and Compassion

Courage and compassion stand at the core of Jedi philosophy, intertwining with the very essence of the Force and guiding those who seek to live a life of purpose. As we delve into these traits, it becomes clear that they are not merely lofty ideals reserved for heroic tales in a galaxy far, far away; rather, they serve as vital tools for transformation, particularly for individuals facing the unique challenges of incarceration.

In the confines of a prison cell, the daily grind can extinguish hope and foster a sense of despair. Yet even in such bleak environments, the seeds of courage and compassion can take root, providing inmates with a pathway to redefine their lives. The archetypal Jedi a symbol of bravery and kindness offers a powerful model for individuals seeking to navigate the complexities of their surroundings and emerge as stronger, more enlightened beings.

Courage

Courage, in its many forms, is often misinterpreted as the absence of fear. On the contrary, true courage means acting *in spite of fear*. For inmates, this might manifest as finding the strength to confront uncomfortable truths about their past behavior, accepting responsibility for their actions, and committing to change. The journey can be daunting, filled with obstacles, internal conflict, and the weight of self-doubt. Yet every act of bravery can serve as a beacon, illuminating the path toward personal growth.

An inspiring example of courage can be found in the story of Marcus, an inmate who faced the consequences of his actions head-on. During his time behind bars, he grappled with the reality of his past a life filled with crime, substance abuse, and broken relationships. One day, while participating in a group therapy session, Marcus took a leap of faith and shared his story. The vulnerability in his voice resonated with others in the room, sparking an honest conversation about accountability and the impact of their choices.

By standing up and sharing his experiences, Marcus exhibited courage born from self-awareness. He did not shy away from the pain of his past; instead, he chose to confront it. This act not only empowered him but also inspired others to open up, creating a communal atmosphere of shared healing. In this way, courage became a catalyst for change, fostering a supportive environment where inmates could acknowledge their struggles and move toward transformation.

Compassion

Compassion, the other pillar of the Jedi ethos, complements courage beautifully. It is the capacity to empathize with others, to understand their struggles, and to extend kindness amidst adversity. In a prison setting, compassion can often feel like a rare commodity, overshadowed by the harsh realities of life behind bars. However, cultivating compassion both toward oneself and others can be a profound means of connection and healing.

Consider the story of Lisa, a female inmate who, during her time in a correctional facility, decided to organize a support group for mothers separated from their children. It was a small gesture that required both courage and compassion, but she was determined to create a space where women could share their fears, regrets, and hopes.

As they sat in a circle, stories flowed each one a testament to the love they had for their children, tinged with the pain of separation. Through this support group, Lisa became a source of strength for others, acting as a compassionate listener. The simple act of being there for one another allowed each woman to feel validated and understood. In turn, they found the courage to be vulnerable and confront their feelings, ultimately creating a sense of community within the prison walls.

Reflection and Practice

By understanding the interplay of courage and compassion, inmates can begin to see themselves not as prisoners defined by past mistakes but as individuals capable of growth and positive change. It is essential, however, that they start this journey of self-discovery by reflecting on their own experiences with these traits.

Encouraging inmates to identify moments in their lives where they exhibited courage or situations where they wished they had shown more compassion can spark deep introspection. This process instills a sense of agency, illuminating the truth that, despite external circumstances, they possess the power to summon these traits from within.

Reflection does not always come easily, especially for those who may have suppressed their emotions for a long time. Therefore, practical exercises can aid in this process. Journaling, for instance, can serve as an invaluable tool. Inmates might write about a time when they felt afraid and how they overcame that fear. They could also explore instances where they offered compassion, even in small ways whether to a fellow inmate, a family member, or themselves.

Another approach involves guided discussions around courage and compassion, utilizing films or literature featuring characters who embody these traits. Inmates can analyze the decisions made by these characters, explore the consequences of their actions, and draw parallels to their own lives. Such discussions can foster a collective understanding that the journey of a Jedi like that of every individual is riddled with challenges but ultimately leads to personal evolution.

A Continuous Journey

As we continue to examine the significance of courage and compassion, it is critical to recognize that these qualities are not isolated. They are connected to the broader themes of redemption and healing that permeate human experience. A key component of the Jedi teachings is the reminder that it is never too late to change one's path.

Just as the Force flows through all living beings, the potential for courage and compassion resides within every individual, waiting to be awakened. This philosophy can unlock a powerful shift in perspective for those in incarceration. Rather than viewing their circumstances as insurmountable barriers, inmates can learn to view their time in prison as an opportunity for reflection, growth, and eventual reintegration into society.

The journey may include setbacks and challenges, but every act of courage even in the face of adversity reinforces resilience. The power of compassion extends beyond mere understanding; it is a call to action. Just as members of the Jedi Order came together to support one another in times of need, inmates can benefit from creating and nurturing networks of mutual aid. These connections provide comfort and encouragement, fostering a sense of belonging that is often missing in the prison environment.

One of the greatest barriers to cultivating both courage and compassion is the sense of isolation that accompanies incarceration. Inmates often feel alienated from their families, their communities, and even from their own identities. By forming supportive alliances within the prison, they can cultivate an atmosphere where courage is celebrated and compassion becomes a collective value.

Additional programs within prisons that focus on mentorship or peer support can further embody the principles of Jedi wisdom. Individuals who have successfully rehabilitated, or who are further along in their journey, can share liberating insights that instill hope in newcomers or those still grappling with their circumstances. Such programs serve not only as a testament to change but also as a means of empowering others, demonstrating the profound impact of kindness in action.

As each inmate engages with the core values of courage and compassion, transformation begins to unfold both internally and externally. The walls that confine them physically start to feel less restrictive as they harness the power of these traits to reshape their identities. It is no longer about being labeled a felon; it becomes about being a warrior of light capable of change and committed to making amends with themselves and those they have wronged.

Enduring the rigors of incarceration can cultivate resilience in those who choose to embark on this path. Challenging circumstances often reveal the depths of one's character, pushing individuals to confront their fears and extend their compassion beyond their own experiences. In many ways, the prison so often perceived as a place of despair can transform into a sanctuary for growth, where the strength of the Force is recognized and celebrated in the mundane acts of everyday courage and kindness.

Ultimately, this journey beckons all to take a step back and consider how courage and compassion play out in their own lives. What does it mean to embrace bravery amidst fear? How can we extend compassion to ourselves and others? By engaging with these questions, we not only harness the power of the Force within ourselves but also empower those around us to rise above their circumstances.

As this subchapter draws to a close, the invitation remains for each reader especially the inmates who find solace in these words: reflect, act, and strive to embody courage and compassion in all aspects of life. The path may be winding, the trials may be many, but with each choice made in the light of these Jedi traits, the possibility of transformation becomes not just a dream but a living reality.

The Journey Ahead

The path before you may seem daunting, but within it lies an expansive universe of possibility much like the vastness of space that the Jedi navigated. The journey of self-discovery is one that each of you has the potential to embark upon, harnessing the wisdom of the Force as a source of strength, guidance, and healing.

In this moment, consider your journey not as an overwhelming cascade of tasks and expectations, but as a series of small, intentional steps leading you toward a deeper understanding of yourself and your capabilities.

The first step is a shift in perspective. You have likely faced trials that shaped your worldview, confining you in definitions that may not represent your true potential. Just as a young Padawan learns from their mistakes, you too can redefine your identity beyond the labels of your current situation. Remember, even the greatest Jedi faced moments of doubt and darkness. What set them apart was their ability to rise again, learning and growing from each experience. Your past does not dictate your future; it can instead serve as a valuable teacher, illuminating lessons you can integrate into your journey.

As you stand on the precipice of this exploration, visualize each lesson as a steppingstone. Your thoughts, emotions, and experiences are intertwined with the Force, and by tuning into this ever-present energy, you can transform every challenge into an opportunity. When faced with doubt or anger, see it not as a setback but as an invitation to delve deeper into your own psyche. To journey into the light, one must first confront the shadows. This does not mean succumbing to them but acknowledging their presence, understanding their origins, and allowing them to guide you toward healing.

The principles of Jedi philosophy encourage mindfulness and awareness integral parts of understanding oneself. As you progress, incorporate practices that foster this connection. Meditation, breathwork, and reflective writing can help transform your thoughts and feelings from sources of turmoil into guides that inform your choices. Each day, take time to pause, sit in silence, and listen. What does the Force say to you? What whispers of insight or encouragement emerge from the stillness?

In cultivating this practice, you honor not only yourself but also your connection to something greater. You are never truly alone in this vast universe; there is always support in the energies that surround you.

Throughout history, the Jedi harnessed the delicate balance between knowledge and intuition. Each encounter with conflict or pain can be viewed through this lens. Learning to embrace emotions rather than suppress them allows you to connect more deeply with your inner self. Emotions are powerful tools they hold the potential to guide you, open your heart, and inform your decisions. The key lies in discerning the difference between being reactive and being responsive.

The Jedi embodied patience and contemplation. When faced with a difficult situation, pause. Take a breath. Before acting, consider the course that aligns most closely with your values and aspirations. This practice nurtures wisdom, transforming even the darkest moments into opportunities for growth and connection.

Yet the journey is not solely about introspection; it also involves connection with others. Jedi were not solitary figures they thrived in community. Human beings, too, are inherently social, and your experience of healing will be enriched by building connections with those around you. Lean into the bonds that form within this space. Share your aspirations, fears, and triumphs. Engage in conversations that uplift you and those within your circle, much like a Jedi bringing light to others amid darkness.

Be open to learning from your peers. Every individual has a unique story and perspective that can deepen your understanding. Mentorship, a vital aspect of the Jedi way, is something you can cultivate here. Seek guidance from those who have walked this path before you, or offer your own experiences to someone who may benefit from your insights. Each interaction nourishes the collective spirit, reinforcing the truth that together, you are stronger.

Find opportunities to join in discussions that inspire hope and positivity. Encourage the idea that no matter what struggles arise, growth is always a real and attainable outcome.

The lessons of compassion and forgiveness are intertwined with the journey of self-discovery. Recognizing their importance is essential as you learn to navigate your own feelings and relationships. Forgiveness is not a weakness; it is a powerful act that liberates the spirit from the burdens of resentment and hurt. As you forgive yourself for past mistakes, the energy once consumed by regret can be redirected toward pursuing your goals with renewed passion. Likewise, extending forgiveness to others fosters peace, allowing relationships to heal and flourish instead of remaining bound by pain.

As we prepare to transition into the practical applications of Jedi wisdom, remember that each chapter you turn represents a new opportunity for growth and understanding. Think of the Force as a living symbol of your hope, resilience, and determination to evolve. The journey of self-discovery is not solitary; like the Jedi, you will learn from the interconnectedness of your experiences with others.

In the chapters ahead, we will explore specific practices rooted in Jedi philosophy, providing a toolkit to foster this transformative experience. You will discover mindfulness techniques, emotional regulation strategies, and frameworks for building meaningful connections within this environment and beyond. Each practice will present challenges, but embrace them as invitations for growth. Just as a Jedi faces adversity with courage and wisdom, approach each new lesson knowing it is a step toward your higher self.

As you embark on this journey, envision your potential unfurling like a blossoming flower, revealing endless possibilities. Embrace your role in this narrative, acknowledging that you possess the power to create change within yourself and those around you.

Remember: you have more strength than you know, more capacity for love than you have yet expressed, and a light within you that, when nurtured and shared, can illuminate even the darkest paths.

The hope of transformation is within your grasp. Stand firm, embrace the teachings that resonate with your spirit, and prepare to forge ahead into the journey that awaits. The Force is strong with you; may it illuminate your way as you take your first steps into a brighter future.

With every action, consider the impact on yourself and the collective, allowing this guidance to foster healing, purpose, and community. Let this journey be one of empowerment and strength, shaping you into the individual you were always meant to be.

The path is yours trust in the Force, and let it unfold before you.

Chapter 2: Shadows of the Cell

The Reality of Confinement

The walls of the prison loom high, a concrete bastion that encloses not only the physical body but the spirit as well. Every morning, as the fluorescent lights flicker to life, the stark reality of confinement settles over the inmates like a heavy blanket. The world outside is lush with colors and sounds, and freedom seems like a distant memory a life existing only in faded photographs and whispered dreams.

Within these walls, time is a tyrant. Each day blends into the next, punctuated only by the clang of metal doors and the hollow echo of footsteps on cold concrete. In the prison yard, an expanse of barren land ringed with chain-link fences, the blaring sounds of distant sirens melt into the background. Inmates shuffle about, forming groups or sitting alone on benches that rattle beneath their weight. Here, despair echoes, mirroring the unbroken rhythm of confinement. The sharp lines of the fence seem to grow sharper in moments of silence, emphasizing the inescapable nature of their reality.

Among these bruised and battered souls, there exists a shared understanding of loss the loss of freedom, family, and, perhaps most hauntingly, the loss of self. The emotional landscape of prison life is complex and often violent, both in its expression and its impact.

Liam, a young man in his twenties, sits on the edge of a bench, his hands resting idle on his knees. His gaze is distant, caught between resignation and anger. He reflects on the days that stretch endlessly before him. Each moment feels like a drop of water in an ocean of despair; each day meticulously stripped of autonomy. The weight of his thoughts bears down heavily. Memories of laughter and warmth feel like cruel illusions phantom echoes of what it means to truly live.

Liam wrestles constantly with the demons of his past. Poor choices, deep-seated wounds, and a lack of guidance linger like shadows, haunting him. In the sterile confines of his cell, he grapples with feelings of worthlessness, surrendering to a spiral of hopelessness. As he stares at the drab gray walls, he wonders if he will ever escape the suffocating cycle of despair.

Inmates are not merely serving time; they are imprisoned by their own thoughts and circumstances. The dread induced by the daily routine becomes a powerful force. Food trays clatter against metal tables during meals that are tasteless and devoid of comfort. Conversations carry unspoken fears: anxiety about parole hearings, the possibility of release, or the uncertainty of returning to a world that now feels estranged and unwelcoming. In these brief moments of gathering, inmates mask their emotions, wearing facades that conceal the cracks beneath. Their laughter, though genuine at times, often feels forced a coping mechanism against the pervasive gloom.

Isabella, serving a long sentence for drug-related offenses, feels trapped in a cycle that seems impossible to break. Each new day begins with the reverberating sounds of the morning call. The squeal of metal shutters pulls her from the shallow sleep that evades her at night. Her heart races at the thought of facing another day in confinement. Standing before the mirror in her shared cell, she confronts the stranger staring back. Sunken eyes and a weary face reveal the weight of her anxiety.

Around her, the clamoring of fellow inmates creates a backdrop of noise that serves as both a comfort and a reminder of their shared predicament. Every interaction is colored by the desperation of survival. In quiet moments, Isabella finds solace in the teachings of the Jedi, reflecting on the power of hope and resilience. The stories she clings to the struggles and triumphs of Jedi knights provide a brief escape from the oppressive nature of prison life. They remind her that even in the darkest times, there exists the possibility of redemption and change. Yet with each passing day, those teachings feel increasingly distant, swallowed by the starkness of her environment.

The isolation can be torturous. Lila, an older inmate, sits alone in the corner of the common area, her body hunched as if the weight of the world rests on her shoulders. Memories of her family feel like fleeting wisps of smoke here one moment and gone the next. Conversations with her children have become painful exercises; each call is a reminder of what she has lost. The love she once took for granted now feels like a distant star, forever out of reach. Frustration and inadequacy take root, feeding a cycle that is hard to break.

Confinement strips away the identities inmates once held dear, leaving them raw and exposed. Each is forced to confront the core of who they are a reality layered with vulnerability and fear. As they navigate the dynamics of prison life, the nuances of friendship, rivalry, and survival lay themselves bare. Bonds are forged through shared experiences, yet they can be broken just as easily. The constant shift of power creates an atmosphere charged with tension, where trust is fragile and the fear of betrayal lingers like an unwanted guest.

Within this harsh landscape, the mind itself can become a formidable adversary. Carlos, a quiet figure who blends into the background, feels trapped by his own thoughts. The echoes of his past his choices, his mistakes, the faces of those he has wronged haunt him relentlessly. His cell is both sanctuary and prison, forcing him to confront the demons within. Hope flickers, only to be extinguished by self-doubt, leaving him wandering through an emotional wasteland. He longs for connection, for someone to break the silence and offer a glimmer of understanding. Yet the fear of vulnerability holds him captive, further binding him in chains of isolation.

The daily rituals of prison life are not merely acts of survival but reflections of the deeper psychological currents running through its walls.

The monotony of routine meals, showers, and programmed activities offers little comfort when weighed against the persistence of despair. As inmates march through the halls, they wear the heavy shroud of expectation, molded by the belief that they are defined by their pasts. The teachings of the Jedi remind them of the power of choice and the control of destiny, yet those ideals often feel like distant stars in a sky obscured by clouds.

Amidst this backdrop of despair, instances of resilience begin to peek through the cracks. In small moments, inmates share glances of understanding nods of camaraderie that briefly transcend their suffering. Conversations hint at growth emerging from adversity: the ability to find purpose even in confinement. These moments serve as reminders that hope can be nurtured, that the spirit can endure despite an oppressive environment.

Within these walls, amidst looming shadows and encroaching darkness, sparks of light flicker into existence connections forged between kindred souls who share in the struggle.

Jordan, a long-term inmate, emerges as a beacon of hope within this stark landscape. He has discovered ways to channel his emotions into creative outlets, transforming pain into poetry and despair into prose. His words carry weight, resonating with those around him during moments of shared struggle. When he recites verses echoing Jedi teachings, something changes: despair loosens its grip, laughter bubbles up amidst shared stories, and inmates are reminded that while confinement may strip away their freedom, it cannot extinguish their spirit.

The act of expression through art, writing, or conversation becomes a lifeline. It allows inmates like Jordan and Isabella to transcend the limitations of their environment, turning experiences of pain into sources of meaning. The power to share their narratives fosters community, a bond that defies the isolating nature of confinement. In these exchanges, they discover that while their physical bodies are contained, the human spirit possesses an innate strength that can flourish even in the shadows.

With each passing day, the cycle of despair begins to shift. Acknowledgment of shared struggles breeds resilience and empathy, slowly unearthing the humanity buried beneath layers of anger and hopelessness. Jedi wisdom patience, perseverance, and faith in the Force intertwines with the reality of prison life, offering tools to reshape destinies. Inmates learn to navigate their emotions their fears, doubts, and desires while challenging the societal narratives that define them solely by their incarceration.

Each encounter, whether a story shared in the common area or a moment of solitude in a cell, carves a new path toward healing. Hope blossoms in unexpected places, forming a bridge across the overwhelming chasm of despair. Through these connections, inmates begin to realize that confinement does not dictate their worth. They hold the power to define themselves beyond the walls that restrain them.

As the narrative of confinement unfolds, it reveals both the darkness and light within human experience. These emotional landscapes painted with shades of despair and splashes of hope challenge the common perception of prison life. The struggle to exist within such confines is both individual and collective, a testament to the resilience of the human spirit.

The lessons of the Jedi become integral to this journey, reminding inmates that even in the face of overwhelming odds, they hold the power to ignite change within themselves and for one another. Together, they learn to navigate the shadows of confinement, united in their quest for understanding and hope. The reality of their situation remains stark, but they begin to forge a path illuminated by the strength of shared experience and the wisdom of the Jedi. Through their struggle, they uncover a truth that transcends prison walls: hope, too, can be a powerful Force capable of transforming despair into possibility.

In the shadows of the cell, a new understanding of life begins to emerge one rooted in the belief that freedom exists not only outside the walls but also within the soul.

Finding Hope in Darkness

In the heart of the deepest darkness, where despair often reigns supreme, lies a glimmering ember of hope waiting to be ignited. The prison cell imposing, confining, and a sheer embodiment of suffocating gloom can also become a crucible for profound transformation. Just as the stars shine brightest against the inky blackness of night, so too can the human spirit discover its potential in the shadowy depths of confinement.

Consider the metaphor of a seed buried beneath layers of earth. To the untrained eye, it may appear lost, buried, and forgotten. Yet within that seed lies the promise of life the instinctual will to push through obstacles and reach for sunlight. Similarly, inmates may find themselves encased in their own layers of darkness and regret, yet within each individual exists dormant potential, waiting to unfold a leap into self-discovery that can illuminate even the dullest confines of existence.

Take the story of Marcus, a former gang member who found himself in maximum-security prison after a series of reckless decisions spiraled out of control. His world was reduced to gray concrete and unforgiving metal, where minutes stretched into hours and days blurred into an endless stream of sameness. Initially, he succumbed to desolation resentment brewing like a storm cloud, blurring his vision of the future.

It wasn't until he stumbled upon a dusty book in the prison library an exploration of philosophy and the nature of hope that his journey began. Like the sudden ignition of a lightsaber in a dark room, the words on the page illuminated his inner world, painting a vision of a future beyond the cell's confines. The realization struck with electrifying intensity: his past did not define him.

He began to write first poetry, then larger narratives of his life. Each word became a step toward healing, a declaration of agency over his own story. In his writings, Marcus expressed not only regret but also the lessons learned. He wrestled with the interplay of light and dark, confronting his choices head-on while envisioning a path to redemption.

This process of self-reflection and expression cracked open the hardened shell of despair. Just as the Jedi learned to harness the Force not only as a weapon but as a means of enlightenment, Marcus began to harness his inner strength recognizing the vast landscape of his potential.

Another story is that of Anna, a young woman incarcerated after a series of unfortunate decisions rooted in addiction. Alone in her cell, the nights felt longest, her dreams teeming with shadows of self-loathing and hopelessness. Yet, in the quietest of moments, Anna found solace in meditation a practice she had once brushed aside in her pre-incarceration life.

Inspired by the principles of mindfulness, she began to witness the breath of each moment, noticing how it ebbed and flowed like tides across a darkened shore. Through meditation, Anna discovered the power of presence, which drew her from the darkness threatening to engulf her. Each session became an exploration of her inner realms, gently cleansing layers of pain and regret that had long weighed her down.

This journey mirrored a Jedi's training, where challenges arise not as barriers but as essential steps toward growth. Just as Jedi must face their own dark side, Anna confronted the ghosts of her past, learning to navigate the labyrinth of her emotions and recognize the flickers of hope buried within.

As her practice deepened, Anna began to visualize not only freedom from her cell but also a vibrant future a life rebuilt with purpose. She created a vision board, decorating her cell with affirmations and images of her aspirations, much like a Jedi's unwavering resolve to strive toward the light. Even within the bleakest confines of prison, she envisioned a life of service to others, especially to those still entrapped by addiction. This glimmer of purpose illuminated her path forward, fueling her transformative journey toward recovery.

The stories of Marcus and Anna intertwine with a broader narrative that resonates across many prisons today: amidst profound despair lies the potential for rebirth. Though the shadows of the cell may feel insurmountable, they can give way to clarity and revelation an invitation to walk toward the light.

The teachings of the Jedi act as a powerful bridge, connecting inmates to their latent virtues. Central to Jedi philosophy is the belief that every challenge presents an opportunity for growth, and every failure, a steppingstone to wisdom. In many ways, this mirrors modern therapeutic approaches, which emphasize resilience and personal agency.

Inmates often carry not only their own burdens but also the collective weight of their communities' generations scarred by cycles of incarceration, addiction, and violence. Against this weight, the cultivation of hope becomes a radical act of resistance.

As narratives of self-discovery emerge, individuals begin to redefine themselves, impacting their communities in turn. They become architects of change, wielding their stories as tools to inspire hope in others still lost in despair.

Hope, both as a concept and as a lived reality, thrives even in darkness. Viktor Frankl, in *Man's Search for Meaning*, argued that the will to find meaning in suffering allows individuals to persevere. This truth underscores not only Jedi teachings but also a universal principle: even in confinement, personal evolution is possible. By embracing the journey inward, inmates can rewrite their narratives, building bridges out of the shadows and into the light.

A vital source of strength lies in community as well. The Jedi Council can serve as a metaphor for the importance of support systems in an inmate's life. Peer groups, family, educators, and counselors all play essential roles in reigniting hope. When individuals feel the support of others much like Jedi bolstered by their Order they are more likely to embrace their potential and strive for a brighter existence.

Consider the transformational power of restorative justice programs. These initiatives foster dialogue between victims and offenders, encouraging healing through understanding. They echo the Jedi's pursuit of balance, harmony, and empathy, offering a platform where inmates can recognize the impact of their actions while also engaging in personal healing and accountability.

The lessons derived from both personal journeys and communal support reveal an essential truth: hope is not mere optimism. It is an active force, an inner courage guiding individuals toward envisioning a better future.

As Yoda reminds us, *"The dark side clouds everything. Impossible to see the future is."* Yet within that cloudiness lies the opportunity for awakening the chance to ignite the flame of hope, which can radiate like a beacon through the shadowed path of self-discovery.

The journey to recovery is deeply personal and multifaceted, entwined with the realization that darkness only amplifies the brilliance of the light. In their respective stories, Marcus and Anna did not simply survive their circumstances; they emerged as warriors champions of resilience armed with the knowledge that they could redefine their destinies, much like a Jedi wielding a lightsaber to cut through the dark.

Having traversed this path, they extended their hands to others still trapped in shadow. As hope took root within them, they shared their narratives with fellow inmates, weaving a tapestry of resilience that inspired collective growth. This shared understanding, rooted in empathy, fostered a familial bond strengthening not only individual resolve but also building a supportive community capable of lighting the way for one another.

Educational and rehabilitation programs that introduce mindfulness, creative writing, and artistic expression further reinforce this transformation. These practices channel energy into constructive outlets, allowing inmates to voice their truths in a world hungry for connection. Such outlets uplift the spirit while cultivating emotional intelligence a crucial element in healing and redemption.

Beyond prison walls, the journey of hope continues into reintegration and beyond. When individuals step back into society after incarceration, the foundation laid during their transformative years becomes a guiding compass. It is essential that society engage with them not from the perspective of past transgressions but from the lens of potential allowing them to continue their narrative of hope and purpose well beyond the prison gates.

For instance, mentorship programs that pair former inmates with community leaders can create meaningful dialogue and a path to reintegration that transcends the simple act of serving a sentence. Much like the relationship between a Jedi and a Padawan, these mentorships enable the sharing of wisdom and experience, allowing others to forge their own paths of light and positivity.

Hope in the darkness is not a simple flicker; it is a powerful force capable of shattering the oppressive silence that often lingers within a cell. Just as Jedi initiates learn to connect with the Force, individuals in prison can learn to connect with their inner strength and resilience. The journey illuminated by hope is rarely smooth; it is often fraught with challenges. Yet it is precisely through navigating those challenges that true self-discovery occurs.

No matter how oppressive the shadows may seem, the potential for growth, change, and recovery exists within each individual. Every inmate can unearth their own journey, using the light of hope to navigate through darkness, much like a Jedi facing the abyss. By embracing the stories of those who found purpose amidst despair, we come to understand that hope not only exists but thrives in the most unexpected places illuminating lives and bridging the gaps carved by fear, shame, and regret.

Finding hope in darkness becomes not just a personal mission but a collective aspiration, an ethos that nurtures resilience and fosters connection. By harnessing the transformative power of hope, we can collectively emerge from the shadows and walk toward a brighter future, guided by the enduring light of self-discovery and purpose. In this dance of shadows and light, the spirit of each individual can soar, embodying the truth that even in the darkest of moments, hope remains a fiercely blooming flower waiting for the right conditions to flourish.

From Shadows to Light

In the dim light of a prison cell, despair often takes root. The shadows that envelop inmates may seem impenetrable, filled with fear, regret, and hopelessness. Yet these shadows are not the end; rather, they can serve as the backdrop against which light shines brighter. Transitioning from these oppressive shadows into the illumination of hope is not just a possibility it is a journey.

It is a journey inspired by the teachings of the Jedi, grounded in principles of resilience, mindfulness, and constructive change. The Force, an energy field that binds and connects all living things, serves as a metaphor for the potential each inmate possesses. No matter how deeply buried beneath the weight of past mistakes or present circumstances, that potential remains waiting to be harnessed and transformed into something powerful.

As inmates begin to recognize their own capacity for change, they can take significant steps toward empowerment and healing. This subchapter seeks to illuminate practical paths to guide them from the shadows of confinement into the light of new possibilities.

The first step in this transformative journey is recognizing one's own feelings and thoughts. Much like a Jedi must attune themselves to the Force within and around them, inmates can cultivate self-awareness. This practice begins with mindfulness, a discipline rooted in both ancient wisdom and modern psychology. Mindfulness encourages individuals to observe their thoughts and emotions non-judgmentally. Instead of becoming overwhelmed by anger, regret, or despair, inmates can learn to acknowledge these feelings as fleeting visitors rather than permanent residents in the mind.

Mindfulness exercises can be introduced in small, manageable steps. For example, inmates might start with just a few minutes of focused breathing each day. By concentrating on the in-breath and out-breath, they anchor themselves in the present moment. With practice, this simple technique can reduce anxiety and foster calm.

Over time, mindfulness can expand to encompass daily activities, inviting inmates to fully engage with the experience of eating, exercising, or even thinking. This awareness illuminates' paths once obscured by shadows, offering clarity and insight.

Another fundamental aspect of moving from shadows to light is the practice of self-compassion. Incarceration often breeds harsh self-judgment, compounding feelings of worthlessness and shame. Yet, just as Jedi are taught to act with kindness and understanding, inmates too can benefit from extending compassion to themselves. Recognizing that mistakes do not define one's worth is a critical step toward growth.

Journaling can be an effective way to cultivate self-compassion. Each day, inmates may set aside time to write not with condemnation, but with curiosity and care. They can document affirmations, moments of gratitude, or reflections on the lessons learned from past choices. By shifting the narrative from self-criticism to self-compassion, they create a nurturing inner environment that supports personal growth.

Still, self-awareness and self-compassion must ultimately lead to action. Just as the Jedi are taught that the Force is not only to be felt but acted upon, inmates must translate insight into tangible change. Setting small, achievable goals becomes a steppingstone from shadows into light. These goals should be specific, realistic, and connected to personal values. For example, an inmate might commit to learning a new skill, exercising regularly, or fostering connection through meaningful conversations. Each accomplishment, however minor, becomes a beacon of progress reminding them that change is not only possible but within reach.

Equally important is the role of community and support. The bonds of solidarity can create spaces where hope thrives. Group participation through book clubs, discussion circles, or workshops centered on personal growth offers opportunities for shared encouragement. In these spaces, inmates can exchange stories and insights, learning from one another's struggles and victories. Inspiration often emerges in unexpected forms, revealing that the path out of the shadows is not meant to be walked alone.

The seeds of change flourish in the fertile ground of education and skill development. Just as a Jedi trains diligently to become a master, inmates can invest in their own learning. Many correctional facilities offer educational programs, vocational training, and access to libraries. Engaging with these opportunities can be a powerful tool for empowerment. Education not only provides knowledge and practical skills but also nurtures a sense of accomplishment and opens doors to new possibilities both during incarceration and after release.

Self-discipline emerges as a vital component in the shift from shadows to light. Jedi principles emphasize self-control, focus, and personal responsibility. Inmates can practice discipline in many aspects of daily life, from maintaining a regular schedule to making healthier choices in diet, exercise, and relationships. Establishing routines creates structure and stability, making the journey of transformation feel less daunting. Developing habits such as daily exercise or dedicating time to personal reflection fosters resilience and instills a sense of purpose.

Importantly, inmates can also explore spiritual practices that resonate with them practices that connect them with deeper meaning. Just as the Jedi turn to the Force for guidance and wisdom, inmates may find strength in their own spiritual beliefs, whether through meditation, prayer, or quiet contemplation. These practices can foster inner peace and provide solace amidst the noise of confinement. By exploring spirituality, individuals can cultivate hope, restore a sense of identity, and envision the person they aspire to become beyond the prison walls.

The path from shadows to light is also illuminated by forgiveness. Forgiveness both of oneself and of others is a transformative act. It frees the heart from the heavy burden of anger and resentment. As Jedi wisdom teaches, letting go of the past creates space for growth, healing, and new beginnings. Though difficult, the process of forgiveness can be initiated through guided reflection or restorative justice practices that allow inmates to confront the impact of their actions on others.

Every journey culminates in a vision for the future. Inmates must inspire themselves to dream again, to reconnect with the image of who they wish to become. Whether through affirmations, vision boards, or spoken aspirations shared with trusted peers, envisioning a positive future provides vital motivation and energy. By imagining the steps needed to achieve these visions, inmates can create practical roadmaps that guide them beyond confinement.

Adopting the role of personal advocate is another step toward the light. Just as Jedi serve as guardians of peace and justice, inmates can advocate for themselves and one another within the correctional system. Taking initiative empowers them to seek resources, engage in meaningful conversations, and push for changes that improve well-being. Collective efforts through committees, projects, or calls for better conditions can build supportive communities and inspire hope for a brighter future.

As each inmate embarks on this path of transformation, it is essential to remember that they are not alone. Every Jedi drew strength from others, working alongside peers and mentors. Similarly, the power of community, mentorship, and support networks can provide encouragement in difficult times. Establishing contact with mentors whether outside volunteers, educators, or supportive staff can offer invaluable guidance and affirmations along the way.

Transitioning from darkness into light requires patience, persistence, and self-love. The enormity of change can feel overwhelming, but it must be embraced step by step. Just as a Jedi does not master the Force overnight, progress in this journey unfolds gradually. Every moment spent in pursuit of growth is a moment of healing, empowerment, and resilience.

In the end, the shadows of confinement do not dictate destiny. By drawing upon Jedi wisdom and blending it with modern strategies for mental and emotional well-being, inmates can embark on a transformative journey from darkness to light. Within reach lies the power to embrace self-awareness, cultivate compassion, set achievable goals, nurture supportive communities, invest in education, practice spirituality, foster forgiveness, envision hope, advocate for change, and embody the resilience of a true Jedi.

Though the path may seem daunting, every small step toward improvement contributes to breaking free from despair. Shadows may linger, but light always shines brighter for those willing to seek it. The journey from the shadows of the cell to the radiance of possibility is one of courage and hope an epic quest for a new beginning where every inmate can, in time, become the hero of their own narrative.

Chapter 3: Empathy: The Jedi's Light

The Importance of Empathy

The teachings of the Jedi emphasize a profound understanding of empathy as a cornerstone of their philosophy. In a galaxy far, far away, Jedi are not merely warriors or guardians; they are sages who foster understanding, transcending divisions of species, culture, and belief. Empathy forms the nucleus of their interactions, guiding them through challenges in ways that uplift not only themselves but also those around them.

Much like the Force that surrounds and binds all living things, empathy connects individuals on fundamental levels, nurturing healing and resilience qualities especially vital for those navigating the emotional complexities of incarceration.

Empathy is more than an emotional response; it is the ability to understand and share the feelings of another. Jedi teachings advocate for this deep sense of connection as a way to recognize the intrinsic value of every individual. In the context of incarceration, acknowledging that each inmate carries a story, a pain, a background, and a potential for growth is vital. This recognition fosters a healing atmosphere where individuals can transform adversity into strength and resilience.

Consider David, an inmate who had spent years in solitary confinement. His early days in isolation were marked by despair, resentment, and loneliness. A turning point came when he began participating in a group therapy session guided by a counselor who embodied empathy rooted in Jedi wisdom. The counselor encouraged inmates to share their experiences without judgment, creating a safe space for vulnerability.

As each man opened up about his struggles, David felt a flicker of hope. He realized he was not alone. The stories reflected grief, loss, and anger, but also triumph, understanding, and the desire for redemption. This exchange of stories became the seed of empathy within the group.

When David listened to another inmate, Marcus, describe a turbulent childhood and the hardships that led him to crime, David reflected on his own life choices. Empathy overcame judgment and resentment, replacing them with compassion. He began to see that neither he nor Marcus was defined solely by mistakes, but by the challenges that shaped their paths.

Over time, this shared emotional engagement evolved into social support. Group discussions grew into a network of encouragement where inmates looked out for one another. David began to feel the heavy weight of loneliness lift. Inspired by Jedi principles of connection, he carried the torch of empathy forward, volunteering to lead sharing circles where others could speak freely. He often described their journey as a walk through the Force a collective path toward healing and self-discovery.

In this context, empathy served a dual purpose: it helped inmates process their own emotions while attuning them to the experiences of those around them. This transformation mirrored the Jedi's relationship with the Force an energy both within and beyond themselves. Just as Jedi harness the Force, inmates began to harness empathy, using it as a powerful tool for healing and growth.

The Jedi teachings of non-judgment and acceptance were especially influential. In a rigid environment where inmates often feel dehumanized and defined by their pasts, the Jedi approach to empathy encourages a different narrative. It empowers individuals to look beyond surface actions to see the person behind the choices. This shift fosters dignity and worth essential ingredients for healing.

The act of empathy allows inmates not only to support one another but also to reconnect with their inner selves, igniting sparks of hope for a different future.

A poignant example of this transformation can be found in Maria, an inmate who once carried deep animosity toward others. She viewed her peers through lenses of fear, rivalry, and preconception. Yet, through peer-led workshops grounded in Jedi philosophy, Maria began to recognize the shared humanity in those around her.

One session changed her perspective completely. She was paired with Luis, a former teacher whose unfortunate circumstances led him to prison. Listening to his heartfelt account of mistakes and regrets, Maria began to recognize her own struggles and feelings of inadequacy. This moment awakened empathy, forging a bond that blossomed into a supportive friendship.

Friendships like these became the backbone of healing within the inmate community. Empathy reshaped Maria's outlook, helping her embrace flaws her own and others with greater compassion. Mindfulness and reflection, central to Jedi practice, began to edge into her daily thoughts. Each interaction became an opportunity for growth. No longer seeing others as rivals, she chose to collaborate, nurture, and support, creating a culture of empathy that spread through the facility.

As empathy flourished, it sparked a broader cultural shift. Informal support networks grew stronger, and mentorship programs emerged where stable inmates helped newcomers navigate emotional challenges. The ripple effect of empathy transformed the prison environment from stark isolation into a sacred space where vulnerability, sharing, and community became standard practice.

Studies highlight that trust and social support play crucial roles in rehabilitation. The feedback loop created through empathy nurtures an environment where people feel safe to admit vulnerabilities, seek help, and support one another. In this sanctuary, Jedi values merged seamlessly with modern therapeutic practices, demonstrating a profound truth: healing occurs in connection, understanding, and community-building.

Furthermore, the stories of growth and resilience that emerge from these experiences underscore the true essence of empathy as taught by the Jedi. Empathy serves as a guide for recognizing the light within oneself and others, illuminating pathways toward reform and personal development. Each story shared in the sacred space of empathy becomes a steppingstone toward healing not only for the individual but also for the collective community of inmates.

By fostering empathy, inmates are encouraged to step outside their own experiences and reflect upon the challenges faced by those around them. This duality creates a far-reaching impact, turning personal hardships into opportunities for compassion-based support. It reshapes perceptions and alleviates the divisions that often exist within correctional facilities, facilitating unity and collective healing across diverse backgrounds.

As inmates embrace the Jedi wisdom of empathy, they gain the knowledge that self-worth does not reside solely in what has been done, but also in the efforts made toward change and understanding. In sympathizing with their peers, they embark on personal journeys of healing, moving beyond the confines of their mistakes. This internal growth aligns closely with the Jedi principles of forgiveness and self-acceptance timeless values that affirm the potential for redemption in every person.

Such transformations, driven by the potency of empathy, are not merely anecdotal. They are substantiated by psychological research highlighting the vital role of emotional intelligence in rehabilitation. By incorporating elements of Jedi teachings into therapeutic programming, inmates are better equipped to navigate their emotional landscapes, forge connections, reduce recidivism, and promote overall well-being.

Empathy nurtures the spirit, enabling individuals to reconstruct their identities beyond the labels imposed upon them. As they foster and channel empathy, inmates become agents of change within themselves, their communities, and the wider world. The profound connection cultivated through empathetic engagement facilitates both recovery and empowerment, embodying the Jedi's legacy: to be a force for good, lighting the path not just for oneself but for all beings.

Ultimately, the journey of healing through empathy parallels the Jedi's pursuit of knowledge and wisdom. By understanding their emotions and embracing the connections forged with others, individuals discover the true power of the light within. This connection rooted in mutual understanding and compassion illuminates the path forward, a path fraught with challenges but rich in promises of hope, redemption, and new beginnings.

Like the Jedi, inmates learn that true strength lies not in combat or conflict, but in the quiet courage to open their hearts, extend compassion, and genuinely connect with those around them. Mastering empathy is akin to wielding a lightsaber with grace: it signifies an embrace of peace, understanding, and the unwavering belief in the potential for transformation.

Empathy Exercises

Empathy is one of the most profound qualities a person can develop, acting as a bridge between individuals and fostering deeper connections that transform communities. For those in the confines of incarceration, empathy can be a crucial element of healing and reintegration.

Drawing from Jedi philosophy, which emphasizes compassion and understanding, this subchapter presents practical exercises designed to cultivate empathy. By engaging in them, inmates can step into the perspectives of others, better understand their struggles, and experience the transformative potential of genuine connection.

These exercises are most effective in group settings, where shared experiences and reflection foster bonds among participants. Through guided discussions and practice, inmates can develop a greater sense of community one that transcends the physical walls of confinement.

Establishing a Safe Space

Before beginning, participants should create a safe and respectful atmosphere. This can be done through an introductory circle where each person shares their name and one personal hope or aspiration. Confidentiality and respect are emphasized to ensure that everyone feels free to speak without fear of judgment.

The Story Exchange

• **Instructions:** Participants pair up and take turns sharing a personal story that had a significant impact on their lives. This could be a moment of pride, joy, failure, or loss.

• **Listener's Role:** The listener must remain silent, giving their full attention and allowing their partner to express themselves without interruption or pressure for feedback.

Guided Reflection: After the exchange, participants consider questions such as:

• What feelings arose as you listened to your partner's story?

• How did it feel to share your own story?

• Were there parts of the story that resonated with your own experiences?

- What did you learn about your partner that you didn't know before?

This reflection builds understanding, revealing commonalities and helping participants see the humanity in one another's experiences.

Group Debrief: The pairs then rejoin the larger group to share insights and reflections. Many discover that truly listening can open the door to another's reality, igniting compassion.

Role Reversal

- **Instructions:** Participants are divided into small groups and given scenarios of conflict. Each person acts out a role, exploring the emotions, motivations, and struggles of the characters.

- **Example Scenarios:**

- A mother struggling to provide for her children after a family loss.

- A person dealing with addiction and its impact on relationships.

- A newcomer to the facility facing ridicule from others.

Groups prepare and then perform their scenes for one another. This exercise fosters perspective-taking, as participants embody experiences beyond their own.

This exercise shines a light on the complexity of emotions, prompting participants to connect with the struggles of the characters they portray.

Guided Reflection

After each performance, the group should reflect together. Guiding questions may include:

- What feelings did you experience while portraying or observing the role?

- How did stepping into another's shoes shift your perspective or understanding of that character's actions?

- What connections can you draw between the role played and your own experiences?

The Empathy Bridge

This activity encourages participants to think beyond themselves and consider their place in the larger community.

- **Step 1: Identifying Issues**: Participants list issues affecting their communities whether within the facility, in their local neighborhoods, or even in broader society.

- **Step 2: Sharing and Discussion**: Each person shares which issue resonates most with them and why. They then form pairs or small groups to discuss how these challenges affect individuals in the community and what emotions might arise from such experiences.

- **Guided Reflection:**

- How do these issues connect to your own experiences?

- What feelings arise when thinking about others facing these challenges?

- What small actions could you take to show empathy toward those affected?

- **Step 3: Action Planning**: Groups work together to create action plans with measurable steps to demonstrate empathy in daily life or within their community. This might include volunteering, supporting others in times of hardship, or advocating for positive changes.

Mindful Observation

In line with the Jedi principle of mindfulness and presence, this exercise helps participants practice awareness of emotions and non-verbal communication.

- **Step 1:** Participants sit in silence and observe those around them whether fellow inmates or staff paying close attention to body language, tone, and facial expressions.

- **Step 2:** Afterward, participants share their observations in small groups, noting emotions they perceived and possible stories beneath the surface.

- **Guided Reflection:**

- How did it feel to be an observer rather than a participant?

- What emotions did you identify in others?

- Did this practice shift your understanding of how others might be feeling?

Empathy in Action

This final exercise asks participants to put empathy into practice.

- **Step 1:** In small groups, participants brainstorm and select one community project to pursue together.

- **Examples:** Organizing a small event, creating informative materials, or offering peer support.

- **Step 2:** Before beginning, groups set goals and discuss the anticipated impact of their project, reinforcing their emotional connection and their commitment to transforming empathy into meaningful action.

Through action, empathy becomes more than a concept it becomes lived practice, creating ripples of positivity that extend beyond confinement.

Throughout these exercises, participants should be reminded that, like mastering a lightsaber, cultivating empathy is a continuous journey requiring patience, intention, and mindfulness. By integrating the Jedi concept of *"seeing through the eyes of others"* into daily life, inmates can begin to break cycles of negative thinking, foster healing, and build collaborative communities.

In conclusion, the exercises outlined here provide practical tools for exploring and strengthening empathy in a supportive environment. By stepping into the shoes of others, reflecting on shared experiences, and turning compassion into action, participants can cultivate deeper human connection, foster bonds that transcend their circumstances, and walk toward a brighter future. In this way, they embody the very essence of what it means to be a Jedi a beacon of light in a world often overshadowed by darkness.

Building a Support Network

At the heart of every community whether a bustling city or a secluded prison lies an indispensable thread that binds its members together: empathy. The Jedi, though fictional, epitomize this deep sense of compassion, serving as timeless reminders of the power of relationships to heal and uplift.

Within the confines of incarceration, building a support network is not merely beneficial it is vital to personal growth, emotional resilience, and collective healing. This subchapter explores the importance of fostering such networks in prison and how shared experiences can facilitate recovery, empowerment, and transformation among inmates.

Navigating the complexities of prison life can be overwhelming. The walls of confinement often come with profound isolation, fear, and despair. For many, the emotional burden of past actions weighs heavily, feeding guilt, shame, and loneliness. In these moments, the value of community becomes unmistakably clear.

Just as Jedi apprentices rely on one another for guidance during training, inmates can turn to each other for strength in their darkest hours. A support network becomes a sanctuary where empathy, respect, and shared understanding can thrive.

At the heart of such a network is the realization that vulnerability can be a strength. Jedi are trained to acknowledge their own feelings and those of others; likewise, inmates can learn to embrace and share their emotions without fear of judgment. This openness fosters trust, allowing individuals to lower their guard and speak candidly about their experiences.

In a prison culture often shaped by stoicism or bravado, vulnerability can spark transformation. When one inmate shares their struggles, it encourages others to do the same dismantling walls of isolation, brick by brick.

Consider, for example, a small group of inmates who gravitated toward one another through their shared experience of addiction. Each bearer of past mistakes, they come together in a shared commitment to confront their demons, seeking not just recovery but a new way of life. In these meetings, they draw strength from their collective journey, validating each other's experiences in ways that could hardly be achieved alone. One inmate might share the story of a relapse, only to find others nodding in understanding rather than judging. Another might recount a moment of weakness that is met not with scorn but with encouragement, as group members remind one another that the journey to rehabilitation is rarely linear.

In recognizing their common humanity, they transform struggles into steppingstones, promoting healing in a supportive and empathetic environment. Empathy flourishes through shared experiences, yet its cultivation within a support network requires intentionality. A culture of empathy must be woven into the very fabric of prison life from administrative policies to the casual relationships formed in common areas.

Educational programs play a pivotal role in this process. Workshops on emotional literacy, conflict resolution, and active listening equip inmates with the skills necessary to engage with one another more effectively. These competencies help them not only support their peers but also articulate their own needs.

The role of prison staff cannot be overlooked. Counselors, psychologists, and correctional officers can model empathy and foster connection by encouraging participation in peer-led groups and activities. When inmates see authority figures promoting connection over isolation, they are more likely to engage in the healing process that comes with mutual support.

Healing, however, is not solely an individual pursuit it is a communal effort. Just as Jedi are guardians of balance in the universe, inmates who engage in mutual support help create equilibrium within their environment. A robust support network operates on the principle that when one person thrives, the entire group elevates. For instance, when an inmate speaks honestly about their struggles and receives guidance, they not only benefit themselves but also set an example for others. This positive feedback loop cultivates resilience, enabling individuals to transform their narrative from despair to hope.

As support networks deepen, empathy extends beyond individual experiences. Inmates often share stories of loss, trauma, or separation from family contexts that, when spoken aloud, deepen bonds and foster belonging. A prisoner grieving the death of a loved one may find solace in the understanding of others who have endured similar pain. The validation that comes from such exchanges fosters sempiternal friendships and provides a sense of belonging essential to healing.

This aligns with the Jedi belief in the interconnectedness of all beings. When inmates view each other's journeys through compassion, they become stakeholders in one another's healing. Lifelong friendships often form in prison, rooted in a shared quest for self-improvement, accountability, and encouragement. As they nurture empathy collectively, inmates reinforce not only their individual reform but also their shared commitment to growth.

There are tangible examples of such initiatives in practice. Many correctional facilities have piloted peer mentoring programs where inmates are trained to support one another in emotional struggles, life skills development, and reentry planning. These programs give inmates purpose, enabling them to contribute positively to their community while also benefiting from the healing power of service.

The impact of such networks extends far beyond the prison walls. As inmates learn empathy and practice collective healing, they prepare themselves for reintegration. When they return to society, they carry with them the skills, resilience, and relationships cultivated during incarceration. Communities that foster support networks yield countless stories of reintegration not only of individuals leaving past mistakes behind but also of people returning with a deepened capacity for compassion and understanding.

Challenges, of course, remain. Institutional culture often resists change, rooted more in punishment than in rehabilitation. Many inmates may fear vulnerability, uncertain if openness will be met with betrayal. Yet with sustained initiatives supported by staff, stakeholders, and restorative practices, culture can change. Emphasizing conflict resolution over punishment and nurturing empathy throughout prison life lays the groundwork for a healthier environment.

As Jedi philosophy reminds us, the strength of the Force lies in unity. When inmates lean on one another, they generate a collective energy that strengthens individual well-being and builds a shared vision of a better future. Each connection nurtures compassion within prison walls, weaving a tapestry of resilience and hope capable of withstanding the trials of confinement.

In conclusion, building a support network within prison serves as a beacon of light amidst darkness. Through shared experiences, empathy blossoms, enabling individuals to transform struggles into opportunities for collective healing. By embracing vulnerability, practicing active listening, and validating each other's experiences, inmates pave the way for deeper relationships that foster inclusion and belonging.

With each bond forged, they gain not only the strength to confront past mistakes but also the ability to emerge from incarceration as more empathetic individuals, ready to contribute positively to the world beyond. In these collective efforts bolstered by the spirit of the Jedi we see the power of empathy ignite change, guiding inmates onto a path of hope, resilience, and renewal.

Chapter 4: Weapons of the Weak

Understanding Inner Struggles

In the confines of incarceration, the daunting silence often amplifies the chaotic noise of the human mind. The walls, built to separate and confine, paradoxically serve as a stage for the internal conflicts that inmates grapple with daily. These inner demons born from past traumas, regrets, and fears become formidable adversaries, manifesting as anger, despair, and worthlessness.

Understanding these struggles is not merely an exercise in psychology; it is a journey into the essence of what it means to be human. Jedi teachings encourage us to confront our inner darkness. The battle between light and dark is not only a galactic struggle but also a profound metaphor for our internal conflicts.

Each inmate faces a unique constellation of demons, but these are not weaknesses to be ashamed of. Instead, they are challenges opportunities for growth and redemption.

The Battle with Addiction

Take, for example, an inmate wrestling with addiction. Substance abuse is rarely a simple choice made in weakness; more often, it is a response to deeper pain neglect during childhood, the trauma of loss, or untreated mental illness. This convergence of suffering creates a relentless cycle of craving and guilt.

As Jedi philosophy teaches, *the fear of loss can lead to suffering.* Those trapped in their own minds are often haunted by memories replaying endlessly. In the battle against addiction, the desire to escape reality manifests in destructive behaviors. It echoes the rhythm of a lightsaber duel: frenetic, desperate, and self-sabotaging.

Every clash of sabers mirrors the inner conflict between the yearning to rise above pain and the lure of momentary relief.

Recognizing addiction as a human struggle, not a personal failure, opens the doorway to healing.

Violence as Survival

Consider also the inmate whose life has been punctuated by violence. It is easy to reduce this person to the label of "criminal," but beneath that surface lies a history of survival in hostile environments. The rage that erupts is often the echo of a lifetime of being unheard, unseen, or marginalized.

Violence, for many, became a learned tool for navigating a world perceived as dangerous. Jedi training emphasizes understanding one's emotions naming them, learning from them, and choosing a path forward. In the same way, inmates must learn to reinterpret violent tendencies not as permanent flaws but as learned responses that can be unlearned.

Programs in emotional literacy, conflict resolution, and trauma-informed care provide the foundation for this transformation. With the right support, even lives once defined by violence can be redirected toward healing.

The Weight of Mental Health

Mental health struggles compound the burdens of prison life. Depression often paralyzes, blinding individuals to the possibility of brighter days ahead like being lost in a suffocating fog where light feels unreachable. Anxiety, too, pushes the mind into spirals of self-doubt and fear, often magnified by the uncertainty of parole or release.

Each whisper of opportunity can trigger panic, sometimes leading to withdrawal from support or even hostility toward others. Yet even in this turmoil, seeds of resilience can be planted. Jedi wisdom reminds us: *fear is the path to the dark side. Fear leads to anger, anger to hate, and hate to suffering.*

Inmates can learn to acknowledge fear without surrendering to it. Through mindfulness and meditation mirroring Jedi practices they can begin to see thoughts as transient, learning to observe them without judgment. Guided meditation, cognitive-behavioral techniques, and peer support groups provide lifelines, helping inmates reclaim agency over their emotions.

At times, simply knowing others share the same battles can be the difference between despair and hope.

The Pain of Isolation

Prison life is also marked by strained or broken relationships. Separation from family intensifies feelings of worthlessness, deepening cycles of destructive behavior. An inmate estranged from loved ones may feel rejected, making it harder to confront personal demons.

Through the lens of Jedi belief, relationships are not only sources of pain but also vessels for healing. Programs centered on family counseling, restorative justice, and group therapy allow inmates to rebuild connections. These initiatives foster forgiveness and understanding, creating space for reconciliation and hope.

The Path of Redemption

Redemption is not a single destination but an ongoing process. Jedi philosophy teaches that every challenge holds an opportunity for growth. Recovery, likewise, is rarely linear. Setbacks are inevitable, but with each step taken, inmates inch closer to the light.

The stories of resilience that emerge from these environments mirror the triumphant arcs of the *Star Wars* saga heroes rising from darkness to reclaim purpose and identity.

Ultimately, building a foundation of understanding one's inner struggles allows inmates to chart their own pathways to healing.

By embracing the Jedi mindset compassion, patience, and courage they can confront their inner demons and take steps toward transformation.

Each individual story, despite its painful elements, holds the potential for remarkable transformation an affirmation that within every shadow lies the possibility of light. Navigating these inner battles will not instantly resolve the complexities of prison life, yet acknowledging them cultivates an environment where hope can thrive.

Addressing emotional health through the resilience of the human spirit is essential to rebuilding lives not only for those incarcerated but for society as a whole. In the broader scheme, enlightened practices inspired by both Jedi philosophy and modern psychology hold the power to transform institutions of confinement into sanctuaries of rehabilitation.

Empathy and understanding serve as the bedrock of this journey, guiding both inmates and those who support them as they navigate their emotional landscapes. Just as Jedi Masters guide their apprentices, mental health professionals can serve as mentors, helping inmates illuminate their paths toward understanding and redemption. Words become powerful lightsabers, slicing through darkness as empathy bridges the gaps left by isolation.

In closing, the inner struggles faced by inmates are not signs of weakness but reflections of the battles we all encounter within ourselves. Understanding these struggles leads to the realization that redemption is possible through confronting inner demons and choosing to embrace the light. Jedi wisdom reminds us of our inherent capacity to rise above challenges, reclaim authorship of our destinies, and ultimately transform adversity into strength.

Turning Struggles into Strengths

In the shadowy recesses of confinement, it is easy for despair to envelop the soul. Inmates often grapple with feelings of anger, resentment, and fear emotions that can feel insurmountable and isolating. Yet, through the lens of Jedi philosophy, these struggles can be reframed not as weaknesses but as sources of strength and opportunities for transformation.

Central to Jedi wisdom is the understanding that emotions, while potent, are tools that can either build or destroy. Embracing this perspective allows us to recognize that every struggle is a chance to grow an invitation to connect with our inner selves and harness the energies of the Force to foster resilience, purpose, and peace.

This subchapter aims to guide you through identifying and reframing your emotional battles, drawing on Jedi principles that encourage strength through struggle.

Step 1: Acknowledge Your Emotions

To embark on this journey, we must first acknowledge and articulate the emotions that weigh heavily on our hearts.

Take a moment to reflect:

- What feelings dominate your days?

- Is it anger at the circumstances that brought you here?

- A sense of despair over lost opportunities?

- Fear of an uncertain future?

Acknowledging these emotions is akin to taking the first step toward the light side of the Force. Jedi are taught that understanding their feelings is crucial to mastering them.

Step 2: Begin an Emotional Inventory

Find a quiet space with a journal or piece of paper. Allow your thoughts to flow freely as you write down the emotions that surface. Don't censor yourself; let the words pour out. As you write, consider:

1.   When do these emotions arise most strongly?

2.   How do they affect your daily life and interactions with others?

3.   What memories or beliefs strip you of your power and contribute to these feelings?

Step 3: Reframe with Jedi Perspective

Once you have laid bare your emotional landscape, it is time to reframe those feelings using Jedi principles.

The first key lesson is the power of perspective. Imagine your struggles as training exercises in a Jedi's journey. Just as a Jedi must confront and learn from their fears whether in the face of danger or personal loss you too can approach your emotions with courage.

•   Each moment of despair can become a lesson in resilience.

•   Each surge of anger can be reframed as an invitation to seek peace and forgiveness.

Step 4: Practice Jedi Mindfulness

Mindfulness, a central Jedi technique, encourages living in the present moment without judgment.

When negative emotions arise, do not fight them; observe them as a Jedi might observe a storm in the galaxy powerful yet temporary.

- Take a few deep breaths and ground yourself.

- Notice the physical sensations tied to your emotions. Are your shoulders tense? Is your heart racing?

- Recognizing how emotions manifest physically is the first step to transforming them.

Mindfulness Meditation Practice:

1. Sit comfortably and close your eyes.

2. Inhale deeply through your nose, filling your lungs.

3. Exhale slowly through your mouth.

4. As thoughts arise, picture them as clouds drifting across the sky. Acknowledge them, but let them pass.

Over time, this practice cultivates detachment from negative emotions and reveals the deeper strengths within.

Step 5: Reframe Struggles into Strengths

After practicing mindfulness, return to your journal. For every negative emotion you listed, write a corresponding lesson or strength it could reveal.

- Anger may drive you to advocate for justice or motivate you to understand conflict more deeply.

- Despair may highlight the importance of resilience and patience.

- Fear may teach courage, showing you how to face uncertainty with determination.

Step 6: Cultivate Gratitude

Another pillar of Jedi philosophy is gratitude the practice of focusing on light even in times of darkness.

Gratitude Practice:

- Write down three things each day you are thankful for.

- These might include a kind gesture from a fellow inmate, opportunities to learn, or simply the chance to reflect.

As gratitude grows, it shifts your perspective, lessening fear and despair. Just as a Jedi turns toward the light, you too can cultivate a mindset of appreciation and hope.

Step 7: Transform Suffering into Service

Leverage the idea of "suffering into service." Jedi often channel their trials into a commitment to others. Similarly, your struggles can become fuel for compassion.

- Anger can be transformed into advocacy.

- Regret can become mentorship for others.

- Pain can inspire you to guide those facing similar battles.

By turning suffering into service, you not only heal yourself but also become a source of light for others.

In the Jedi tradition, personal sacrifice often leads to the greater good. Consider how your own struggles could be transformed into opportunities to uplift others. Engage in community outreach, mentorship, or support groups where you can share your experiences and provide guidance to your peers. When we shift focus from our own problems to helping others navigate theirs, we reinforce our strengths and develop a deeper sense of purpose.

As we continue exploring the transformation of struggle into strength, it is essential to understand the importance of support networks. Jedi do not journey alone; they rely on comrades for guidance and encouragement. Within the confines of a facility, you can build connections by participating in group sessions, sharing stories, and listening to the experiences of others. Surrounding yourself with supportive individuals creates a ripple effect when you witness others confronting and overcoming their struggles, it can inspire you to do the same.

Engage in meaningful conversations: discuss the emotions you've been grappling with and explore how others have reframed their challenges. Set goals together and hold one another accountable. This camaraderie can unlock dimensions of strength and resilience that remain dormant when faced in isolation.

Alongside these group efforts, practice self-compassion. Jedi philosophy emphasizes the necessity of embracing imperfections. As you work through emotional battles, remind yourself that growth is not linear. Just as the path of the Jedi involves setbacks, so too does the journey of self-improvement. When you falter, do not berate yourself. Instead, extend the same kindness you would offer a friend. One powerful exercise is to write a letter of compassion to yourself acknowledge your struggles, affirm your worthiness, and remind yourself of your ability to heal and grow.

To consolidate these teachings into actionable steps, commit to a Strength Lab over the next several weeks. Experiment with the following practices, each designed to fortify emotional resilience:

1. **Emotional Inventory**:Continue reflecting on your emotions weekly. Update your journal and note any new feelings or patterns that arise.

2. **Mindfulness Meditation**: Dedicate a few minutes each day to meditation, expanding your ability to observe and detach from negative emotions.

3. **Gratitude Practice**: Write down three things daily that you are thankful for, and whenever possible, express gratitude to others.

4. **Acts of Service**: Identify one way each week to help another inmate whether by offering encouragement, sharing resources, or participating in group initiatives.

5. **Support Network**: Attend group discussions, initiate conversations with peers, and build connections with those on similar journeys.

6. **Self-Compassion Letters**: Regularly write letters to yourself celebrating progress and offering forgiveness for moments of struggle.

By integrating these practices, you will gradually transform struggles into steppingstones of growth.

As you commit to turning struggles into strengths, let Jedi principles illuminate your path. Through mindfulness, gratitude, service, and community, you will discover that the burdens you carry can become tools of empowerment.

Remember: becoming a Jedi in your own life requires patience and practice. Emotional growth is like honing lightsaber skills it demands dedication and persistence. With each victory, no matter how small, you become more attuned to the Force that unites us all.

Each challenge faced is an opportunity in disguise. Quiet your mind and listen closely to the whispers of the Force. It will guide you toward your greatest potential, helping you emerge from the dark corridors of your past as a beacon of healing and hope for yourself and for those who share this journey with you.

The Power Within

In every soul lies a spark a unique light that can guide even the lost through the darkest of times. This spark, often overshadowed by life's challenges and adversities, is what we call the power within. Recognizing and embracing this inner strength is essential for growth, especially for those navigating the turbulent waters of incarceration.

The idea of inner power draws inspiration from the heart of Jedi philosophy. The Jedi believe in the Force an energy that connects all living things and allows individuals to harness their potential. This concept resonates deeply in the prison context. In an environment where control is often stripped away, finding inner power becomes a personal rebellion against despair.

Consider the daily trials faced by inmates: confinement, loss of autonomy, and separation from loved ones. These hardships weigh heavily on the psyche, leading to hopelessness. Yet within these very challenges, the power within can flourish. Just as the Jedi confront the Dark Side, individuals can learn to acknowledge their struggles and grow stronger in the process.

Recognizing one's adversities is not weakness it is the first step toward growth. Facing adversity is like standing at the edge of an immense chasm: the leap appears daunting, and the fear of failure can paralyze even the bravest spirit. But the leap is not about guaranteed success; it is about faith and willingness.

The Jedi teach us to embrace our fears rather than run from them. Similarly, inmates can learn that by acknowledging challenges, they reveal their true potential.

The metaphor of the dark night is powerful here. Every person experiences nights when hope feels out of reach. Yet, just as night is followed by dawn, so too can adversity give way to growth and enlightenment. Darkness has its place; it provides the contrast that makes the light visible. Without night, the brilliance of day would not be appreciated.

This journey is not only individual it is also collective. The Jedi thrive not just as individuals but as a unified Order, bound together by the Force. In prison, the same principle applies. Building supportive communities creates spaces where burdens can be shared and strengths celebrated.

When individuals come together to acknowledge their struggles and lift each other up, the spark of the power within burns brighter both for the individual and for the group as a whole.

This shared experience provides encouragement and hope, creating a sense of belonging among those who may otherwise feel isolated and forgotten. When inmates align their personal journeys with the realization that others walk similar paths, they cultivate resilience and recognize the richness of their collective strength.

This journey toward self-empowerment encourages inmates to seek tools and strategies that help them tap into their inner power. Mindfulness practices, akin to the meditative techniques employed by the Jedi, can serve as essential tools. Such practices foster awareness of one's thoughts and emotions, enabling individuals to confront fears rather than suppress them. Moments of anxiety can thus be transformed into opportunities for reflection and growth.

Equally important is the act of setting achievable goals. Much like a Jedi progresses through stages of training, incremental objectives help individuals build confidence and sustain motivation. Each small victory contributes to the larger narrative of empowerment. Over time, this roadmap of progress becomes a powerful testament to resilience.

The art of storytelling also plays a vital role. Stories connect individuals, providing context, understanding, and a reminder that struggles are universal. Sharing experiences through writing, group discussions, or creative expression helps inmates feel seen and heard. This cathartic process not only fosters personal healing but also inspires others to recognize their own strengths within the shared human experience.

As change unfolds, it is essential to embrace forgiveness both of oneself and of others. Jedi wisdom emphasizes compassion and understanding. For inmates, holding onto resentment can feel like carrying an ever-increasing burden. Forgiveness releases that weight and opens the door to new possibilities. By choosing forgiveness, individuals reclaim their narratives and affirm their rightful place in the continuum of life.

True resilience is not merely the ability to endure, but the ability to thrive amid challenges. Each hardship becomes a steppingstone; each setback, a lesson. Just as the Jedi learn from every encounter, inmates too can cultivate this mindset of growth. Failure is no longer seen as a definitive end, but as a vital component of the journey forward.

Understanding one's inner power also creates an opportunity to craft a greater purpose. Inmates often reflect on future aspirations who they want to become, and how they might contribute to society after release. Defining such a purpose breeds passion, transforming the mundane into a proactive pursuit of greatness. Just as Jedi dedicate their lives to serving and protecting, inmates can aspire to contribute positively to the world around them.

With each step forward, every individual shines a unique light, becoming a beacon of hope amid the shadows. The power within is not ignited by belief alone, but through deliberate action and intent. By facing their struggles directly, inmates reclaim their narratives, reshaping identities once defined by society's labels into identities authored by their own choices.

In the end, every struggle serves as a catalyst for growth. Embracing challenges rather than running from them allows for development that extends far beyond the confines of prison walls. The path toward redemption is rarely linear, nor is it free of fear and uncertainty. Yet when illuminated by the understanding of one's inner strength, hope can be kindled even in the darkest of nights.

Here lies the essence of Jedi wisdom: the true weapon against despair is belief in oneself. Inmates are called to become masters of their destinies, wielding their inner power to carve paths of healing, restoration, and hope. Each person possesses the capacity to emerge from struggle transformed not only as survivors, but as thrivers who illuminate the world around them.

Ultimately, the power within has the potential to ignite change not only for the individual but for entire communities and beyond. In a world where dark nights loom large, it is the collective light of individuals embracing their inner strength that illuminates the path forward.

In recognizing and nurturing this light, inmates are empowered to embark on journeys of healing, compassion, and renewal. As the dawn breaks after the darkest night, so too can each person rise ready to embrace the limitless possibilities that await.

Chapter 5: Mindfulness in the Trenches

The Art of Mindfulness

Mindfulness is an essential practice that resonates deeply with the teachings of the Jedi, who advocate for awareness, presence, and emotional regulation. Within incarceration, mindfulness emerges not only as a therapeutic tool but also as a philosophy that enables a more meaningful engagement with life.

At its core, mindfulness is the ability to maintain moment-to-moment awareness of our thoughts, feelings, bodily sensations, and environment. To practice mindfulness is to cultivate clarity and calm even amid chaos a quality highly prized by Jedi Knights. This clarity creates space for thoughtful responses rather than reactive behavior. For inmates, mindfulness can transform the way they relate to their emotions, allowing them to confront anger, anxiety, or despair with greater equanimity.

The benefits of mindfulness on cognitive function are well documented. Research in psychology and neuroscience shows that regular practice enhances attention span, improves concentration, fosters emotional regulation, and builds resilience against stress.

For inmates who often experience elevated stress due to confinement and uncertainty developing focus and emotional control becomes even more crucial. Through mindfulness, they can expand their capacity for self-reflection and thoughtful decision-making, both vital for personal growth and conflict resolution.

Jedi teachings emphasize self-awareness, urging individuals to look inward and understand their motivations. Mindfulness similarly invites practitioners to explore thoughts and feelings without judgment. This self-inquiry allows inmates to uncover the triggers behind emotional responses, dismantle limiting beliefs, and release destructive habits.

Mindfulness also nurtures compassion. Inmates can learn to extend kindness toward themselves, acknowledging struggles without condemnation much like a Jedi accepts vulnerability as part of growth.

Prison environments are filled with distractions: noise, rigid routines, and constant supervision. Mindfulness offers an anchor in this storm, a way to find calm within chaos. Techniques such as focused breathing, body scans, or mindful observation allow inmates to regain a sense of presence. Even a simple pause to focus on one's breath can create a vital moment of space between impulse and action an essential skill for those seeking peace instead of conflict.

Mindfulness can be practiced individually or in groups. In a group setting, shared practice builds camaraderie and mutual support. Participants who discuss insights and challenges create bonds that help alleviate isolation. This collective effort strengthens the social fabric of the prison environment, transforming mindfulness into both a personal and communal practice.

Mindfulness also supports trauma recovery, a need prevalent in many prison populations. Individuals who have lived through instability, violence, or loss often carry the weight of unresolved pain. Mindfulness provides a safe emotional space where they can confront these experiences with less reactivity, gradually reclaiming their narratives and sense of agency. This mirrors the Jedi path: facing fear directly and embracing the journey, however difficult it may be.

Like any skill, mindfulness requires patience and practice. Just as Jedi undergo years of rigorous training to master their abilities, so too must mindfulness be cultivated consistently. Inmates may face days of distraction or emotional upheaval, but by returning again and again to their practice, they embody the Jedi principle of perseverance. Mastery emerges not from perfection but from persistence and self-compassion.

The benefits of mindfulness extend beyond individuals to the prison community at large. As more inmates engage in practice, the collective atmosphere shifts. Presence and emotional regulation reduce conflict, increase respect, and foster an environment where healing feels possible.

Integrating mindfulness into rehabilitation programs also prepares inmates for reintegration into society. Returning to the community often evokes fear and uncertainty; mindfulness equips individuals with tools to face these challenges with greater resilience. Anchored in self-awareness, they can move forward with clarity and purpose.

The relationship between Jedi wisdom and mindfulness is clear. Jedi teachings encourage holistic well-being, emphasizing emotional balance and wise engagement with the world. In prison, mindfulness becomes the bridge between ancient wisdom and contemporary mental health practices. This synergy not only supports individual healing but also contributes to collective transformation within correctional institutions.

Mindfulness is both an art and a discipline, deeply rooted in Jedi philosophy. It equips individuals to maintain clarity amid chaos, regulate emotions, and strengthen relationships. For inmates, it becomes a pathway to growth, resilience, and healing.

As they cultivate mindfulness, they engage in the noble pursuit of becoming Jedi in their own lives guided not by lightsabers, but by the quiet strength of awareness, compassion, and presence. In doing so, they embody the timeless truth that redemption and transformation lie within reach of all who choose to walk the path of light.

Meditation Techniques

As we delve deeper into mindfulness, we recognize its pivotal role in achieving emotional and mental stability. For inmates, meditation can serve as a sanctuary a way to find peace within the confines of daily realities. Drawing from the teachings of the Jedi, who understood the importance of mind and spirit in cultivating balance, meditation becomes a means of fostering healing, resilience, and harmony.

This subchapter explores a variety of meditation techniques that can be easily adapted to the prison environment. Each method reflects core tenets of Jedi philosophy: mindfulness, awareness, and compassion. The goal is to provide practical tools that inmates can weave into their daily routines, allowing them to foster mental wellness even in restrictive circumstances.

Creating a Foundation

Before beginning any meditation practice, it helps to establish a foundation. Jedi teachings emphasize presence being fully aware of surroundings, thoughts, and feelings.

In prison, this might mean finding a quiet corner or, when that is not possible, learning to cultivate calm even amidst chaos. By preparing oneself intentionally, any environment can become a space for reflection.

Mindful Breathing

One of the simplest and most effective practices is **mindful breathing**, which centers both mind and body.

1. **Find Your Space**: Sit or lie comfortably. Close your eyes, or maintain a soft gaze.

2. **Focus on Your Breath**: Notice the rhythm of your inhale and exhale without trying to control it.

3.   **Count Your Breaths**: Inhale for four counts, hold for four, exhale for four. Repeat several cycles, allowing relaxation to deepen.

4.   **Acknowledge Thoughts**: When thoughts arise, observe them without judgment and gently return attention to your breath.

5.   **Expand Awareness**: After several minutes, broaden awareness to bodily sensations and the surrounding environment while staying anchored in your breathing.

This practice can be used at any time especially during moments of stress or conflict to create calm and clarity.

Body Scan Meditation

The **body scan** enhances awareness of physical sensations and helps release tension, aligning with Jedi wisdom about the connection between body and mind.

1.   **Position Yourself Comfortably**: Sit or lie down and close your eyes if comfortable.

2.   **Begin at the Crown**: Bring awareness to the top of your head. Notice sensations tension, warmth, or stillness.

3.   **Move Downward**: Slowly shift focus through your face, neck, shoulders, arms, torso, legs, and toes.

4.   **Release Tension**: As you encounter tightness, imagine the Force flowing through those areas, softening and releasing tension with each breath.

5.   **Reflect**: When finished, take a moment to observe how your body feels, noting the relationship between your physical and emotional states.

This method is particularly effective before sleep, helping the body and mind relax.

Loving-Kindness Meditation

Compassion lies at the heart of Jedi wisdom. **Loving-kindness meditation** (also known as *metta*) cultivates empathy and forgiveness toward oneself and others.

1. **Settle Into Silence**: Sit comfortably, hands resting in your lap or on your knees. Breathe deeply.

2. **Begin with Yourself**: Silently repeat: *"May I be happy. May I be healthy. May I be safe. May I live with ease."*

3. **Expand Gradually**: Extend these wishes outward to loved ones, acquaintances, those in conflict with you, and eventually to all beings.

4. **Visualize Light**: Picture a warm light surrounding each person, carrying your good wishes.

5. **Acknowledge Emotions**: Difficult feelings may arise. Notice them, allow them to pass, and return to the phrases of compassion.

This practice can transform perspectives, encouraging forgiveness and reinforcing community bonds.

Guided Meditation

For those new to practice, **guided meditations** provide structure and support. They may focus on themes like healing, gratitude, release, or connection to the Force.

1. **Choose Wisely**: Use recordings, scripts, or audiobooks (if available) that promote peace and positivity.

2.   **Create a Routine**: Dedicate a consistent time each day to guided meditation.

3.   **Clear Your Mind**: Follow the guide's instructions closely, setting aside distractions.

4.   **Reflect Afterwards**: Spend a few moments journaling or noting insights that arose.

Guided meditations are especially helpful for beginners, offering a steady framework for developing inner calm.

Walking Meditation

Not all meditation requires stillness. **Walking meditation** combines mindfulness with movement, reflecting the Jedi philosophy of being present in every action.

1.   **Select a Path**: Find a safe, clear area to walk, even if small.

2.   **Synchronize Steps and Breath**: Inhale as you lift your foot, exhale as you place it down.

3.   **Engage the Senses**: Notice the ground beneath your feet, the air around you, the sounds in your environment.

4.   **Return to Focus**: If thoughts distract you, gently bring attention back to walking and breathing.

5.   **Pause to Reflect**: After 10–15 minutes, stop and acknowledge the sense of presence you cultivated.

This moving practice is a powerful way to release stress and sharpen awareness.

Everyday Mindfulness

Beyond structured meditation, inmates can integrate mindfulness into daily life, embodying the Jedi principle of presence in all things:

- **Mindful Eating**: Focus on the taste, texture, and aroma of food. Eat slowly, appreciating nourishment.

- **Mindful Listening**: Listen fully in conversation, without planning a response, cultivating empathy and connection.

- **Mindful Action**: Approach daily routines cleaning, exercising, or working as opportunities for meditation in motion.

- **Transitions**: Use natural pauses in the day (before meals, after work) to pause, breathe, and reset.

- **End-of-Day Reflection**: Each night, recall moments of gratitude or mindfulness, and set an intention for tomorrow.

By embracing a range of meditation techniques, inmates can adopt a proactive approach to mental health. These practices, grounded in Jedi wisdom, offer pathways to inner peace, resilience, and healing.

Meditation empowers individuals to navigate their emotional landscapes with clarity, turning confinement into an opportunity for self-discovery and growth. With regular practice, even the most restrictive environment can become a training ground where the Force guides them toward renewal and strength.

Mindfulness in Everyday Life

Mindfulness is often perceived as something practiced only in quiet meditation a concept that can feel remote from the daily complexities of prison life. Yet mindfulness is not merely an isolated practice; it is a way of being that can be woven seamlessly into everyday activities.

In this subchapter, we explore how mindfulness transcends formal practice to become a constant companion throughout daily interactions and self-reflection. We will examine practical strategies for staying present in various situations, showing how even small moments of awareness can inspire profound changes in behavior and mindset.

At its core, mindfulness is the practice of being present fully engaged in the current moment without judgment. For inmates, who often grapple with past regrets and future anxieties, mindfulness can be transformative. It allows individuals to find solace in the present and draw on Jedi wisdom, using the Force as guidance through daily challenges.

Mindfulness in Interactions

Every conversation, no matter how ordinary, is an opportunity for connection and growth. When approached with genuine presence, interactions become moments of understanding rather than conflict. Consider these practical ways to cultivate mindfulness in daily relationships:

1. **Active Listening**: Focus fully on the speaker instead of preparing your response. Pay attention to their words, tone, and body language. Reflect briefly before replying so your response is meaningful and empathetic.

2. **Mindful Body Language**: Maintain open, relaxed posture. Eye contact, nodding, or leaning slightly forward communicates receptiveness and engagement, fostering trust and connection.

3. **Pause Before Responding**: In moments of tension, take a brief pause. This allows space for thoughtful responses rather than impulsive reactions, preventing misunderstandings and bringing calm to heated situations.

4. **Mindfulness in Conflict Resolution**: Conflicts are inevitable, especially in close quarters. When disagreements arise, acknowledge emotions both yours and others' without reacting defensively. Approach resolution with understanding, not hostility.

5. **Cultivating Empathy**: Practice seeing situations from another's perspective. Consider their struggles, motives, and emotions. Empathy diffuses tension, promotes compassion, and contributes to a more harmonious environment.

Mindfulness in Self-Reflection

Moments of mindfulness also lead inward, creating space for self-awareness and growth. By reflecting consciously, inmates can identify patterns, beliefs, and triggers that shape their reactions. Here are several strategies for mindful self-reflection:

1. **Journaling**: Write daily about thoughts, emotions, and experiences. Explore how past patterns influence present reactions. Journaling fosters clarity and builds agency over one's choices.

2. **Mindful Breathing**: Spend time each day focusing on the natural rhythm of your breath. Acknowledge thoughts without judgment and gently return to the breath. This anchors you in the present and builds emotional regulation.

3. **Setting Daily Intentions**: Begin the day with a mindful intention, such as: *"I will practice patience in difficult situations"* or *"I choose empathy in my conversations."* Check in throughout the day to see how well your actions align.

4. **Body Scan Meditation**: Slowly bring awareness to each part of the body, from toes to head. Notice tension or discomfort without judgment. This practice strengthens the mind-body connection and deepens emotional awareness.

5.   **Evening Reflection**: At day's end, review experiences mindfully. Consider what you learned, how you responded, and areas for growth. Recognizing patterns encourages accountability and intentional change.

The Transformative Potential

When mindfulness is integrated into daily life, its potential for transformation becomes clear. We become more aware of our thoughts, feelings, and reactions, empowering ourselves to choose responses rather than be ruled by impulses.

This is where Jedi wisdom resonates most strongly. Self-awareness, emotional balance, and compassionate action hallmarks of the Jedi mirror the essence of a mindful life.

In the prison context, mindfulness acts as an anchor. Amid pressure, tension, and constant interactions, it provides tools to navigate challenges with calm and intention. Meaningful conversations and mindful reflection build a culture of compassion, turning isolation into connection and fear into resilience.

The journey of mindfulness is ongoing. It requires practice, patience, and commitment. But each mindful breath, pause, and reflection honors both Jedi teachings and the human capacity for growth.

Mindfulness is not limited to formal meditation or moments of solitude. It is a vibrant way of living that can infuse every interaction and every reflection. By bringing presence into conversations, empathy into conflicts, and awareness into daily life, we become architects of our own reality.

Through mindfulness, inmates can forge meaningful connections, cultivate understanding, and nurture profound personal transformation. With the wisdom of the Jedi as a guide, mindfulness becomes more than practice it becomes a way of being, a steady light in the midst of challenge, and a reminder that the Force is always with us.

Chapter 6: Hope: The Galaxy's Oasis

Cultivating Hope

In the vast expanse of the universe, stars shine even in the deepest darkness, illuminating the night and reminding us that hope exists even in the bleakest environments. This metaphor perfectly reflects the importance of cultivating hope, particularly within incarceration.

For inmates, daily struggles can feel like traversing a shadowy galaxy where despair looms as a constant force. Yet, just as stars are born from cosmic dust, hope can emerge from adversity, providing the emotional sustenance needed to endure confinement. The beauty of nurturing hope lies in its power to foster resilience the quality that allows individuals to rise above circumstances, adapt, and even thrive amid difficulty.

Hope acts as a beacon, guiding individuals to set their sights beyond present hardships toward a brighter future. In prisons, where hopelessness can feel all-consuming, cultivating hope becomes pivotal to promoting emotional well-being. It enables inmates to derive strength from within, fostering a sense of purpose and meaning even when their bodies and spirits feel confined.

The Psychology of Hope

Research underscores the profound impact of hope on mental health. Studies consistently show that higher levels of hope are linked to lower rates of anxiety, depression, and suicidal ideation.

For example, a study in the *Journal of Clinical Psychology* found that individuals with greater hope levels were better equipped to cope with stress and trauma, leading to improved psychological outcomes and life satisfaction. Similarly, research in the *International Journal of Behavioral Medicine* revealed that hope acts as a protective factor, buffering the effects of adversity and environmental stressors.

Hope, then, is more than an abstract ideal; it is emotional nourishment. It fuels resilience by shaping one's cognitive framework, promoting a mindset focused on possibilities and solutions rather than problems and limitations.

Hope in Jedi Philosophy

In the world of the Jedi, hope is intertwined with faith the belief in oneself and in the future. This message resonates deeply with inmates, many of whom feel adrift in a galaxy of uncertainty.

Like Jedi who draw strength from the Force, inmates can learn to connect with their inner resources, sparking hope that ignites transformation even within prison walls.

Peer Support as a Source of Hope

Peer support is vital in cultivating hope. Sharing stories, struggles, and victories allows inmates to realize they are not alone. Group discussions offer safe spaces where individuals express their feelings and learn from one another's experiences.

As they encourage each other, they become stars in their own right each story of survival and strength illuminating the path for others.

One inmate reflected:

"When I first got here, I thought there was no way out. I felt like a black hole, pulling everything good away from me. But then I found a group of guys who encouraged me to think differently. They helped me realize that just because I'm inside these walls doesn't mean I can't dream."

This sentiment captures the essence of hope: the ability to envision a future filled with possibility, even when the present feels grim.

Hope's Ripple Effect

Hope not only transforms individuals; it reshapes prison culture. An atmosphere that nurtures hope can reduce conflict, improve relationships, and create a safer, more supportive environment.

Research shows that when inmates engage in hope-centered programs through education, mentoring, or creative expression disciplinary issues decrease and cooperation increases. Such programs provide structure, purpose, and a collective sense of possibility.

Beyond the walls, hope fuels reintegration. Inmates who maintain ties with families, mentors, or community organizations often transition more successfully into society. Programs that connect inmates with supportive networks encourage them to envision a path beyond confinement, filled with purpose and contribution.

Mindfulness and the Jedi Path

Mindfulness practices are powerful allies in cultivating hope. By focusing on the present moment through breathwork, meditation, or stillness individuals can rediscover calmness amid chaos.

Jedi wisdom reinforces this truth. Just as Jedi learn to channel their emotions into strength rather than destruction, inmates can transform despair into hope. Vulnerability becomes a source of resilience, not weakness.

The galaxy itself offers a reminder: even in the endless void of space, stars shine brightly. Likewise, hope can be found in small victories moments of kindness, acts of connection, or steps toward healing all of which glow like constellations in the darkness.

Practical Pathways to Hope

Cultivating hope requires intentional practices. Programs such as **Cognitive Behavioral Therapy (CBT)** can reinforce belief in personal change, while **goal-setting workshops** equip inmates to chart paths toward the future.

A study in the *Journal of Human Behavior in the Social Environment* found that inmates participating in structured goal-setting exercises reported significantly higher hope levels. Like charting a course through the stars, identifying specific, achievable goals creates a roadmap to possibility.

Creative outlets writing, art, and music also provide pathways to hope. Storytelling, in particular, allows individuals to process struggles while reflecting on strengths and aspirations. Each personal narrative becomes part of a larger constellation of resilience, illuminating both individual and collective journeys.

A Galaxy of Possibilities

As inmates cultivate hope and reject the idea that they are defined by their past, new galaxies of possibility begin to unfold. Each individual has the potential to become a bright star lighting the way for others, advocating for mental health, and fostering dialogue about justice and healing.

For mental health practitioners, correctional staff, and community supporters, promoting hope must be central to rehabilitation. Encouraging emotional expression, fostering connections, and instilling purpose can spark transformation that radiates beyond prison walls.

Just as stars once guided weary travelers across the night sky, hope can guide inmates on their journey of recovery reminding them that the power to create meaningful lives resides within.

Cultivating hope within prisons is essential for emotional well-being and resilience. Metaphors of galaxies and stars remind us of the beauty of nurturing hope amid darkness. Empirical studies and personal testimonies affirm its role in mental health and personal transformation.

By embracing hope, fostering peer support, and integrating structured programs, we empower inmates to reframe their lives not as stories of despair, but as narratives of resilience and renewal.

Like stars that persist through the void of space, hope shines even in confinement, guiding individuals toward brighter futures. It is a reminder that even in the darkest of times, light not only exists it thrives.

Vision Crafting

In the vast expanse of the galaxy, every star shines with potential, reminding us that hope persists even in the darkest of times. For many inmates, the reality of confinement can dim their brightest aspirations, veiling the dreams that once guided them.

This subchapter invites readers into the practice of **vision crafting** a soul-nourishing process that helps inmates articulate their hopes and dreams for the future. By drawing on Jedi wisdom and modern psychology, vision crafting becomes an interactive framework that inspires individuals to visualize their desired futures and motivates them to take actionable steps toward achieving their goals.

The Force, an omnipresent energy that flows through all living things, serves as a powerful metaphor. Just as Jedi harness the Force to bring balance, inmates can harness their inner strength to craft visions that resonate with their deepest desires. Vision crafting is about reflection, imagination, and creation drawing from one's unique background, strengths, and aspirations.

Preparing for the Journey

To begin this process, it is vital to create space for reflection. Within the confines of prison routines, self-exploration is often difficult. The first step, therefore, is establishing a safe mental and physical environment where the mind can wander and the heart can dare to dream.

This might mean gathering in small groups or finding solitary quiet time during the day. Ideally, the environment should mirror the tranquility of a Jedi training hall: calm, with limited distractions and a sense of sacred purpose.

Exercise 1: Guided Meditation

Start with a guided meditation to calm the mind and open the heart.

- Instruct participants to sit or lie comfortably.

- Guide their breathing: inhale deeply, exhale tension.

- As their rhythm settles, invite them to visualize a serene sanctuary free from current struggles, filled with hope and possibility.

- Encourage them to immerse themselves in the colors, sounds, and sensations of this imagined world, allowing the vision of a brighter future to take shape.

Exercise 2: Crafting the Vision

After meditation, guide participants into creating their personal vision.

- Provide art supplies such as paper, pencils, or markers.

- Invite them to design **vision boards** that reflect their aspirations covering areas like career, relationships, health, and personal growth.

- Encourage creativity without limits, using images, words, and symbols that resonate with their dreams.

Each stroke of color or word added becomes a step closer to a desired future. Just as Jedi rely on imagination to foresee possibilities, inmates can give tangible form to their aspirations.

Exercise 3: Verbal Sharing

Once the vision boards are complete, bring participants together for a **sharing circle**.

- Each inmate describes their board, explaining why their vision matters.

- Listening to others' aspirations fosters connection, accountability, and camaraderie.

This communal exchange demonstrates that dreams are not solitary endeavors. By articulating visions aloud, individuals strengthen both their personal commitment and their bonds with peers.

Exercise 4: Setting Intentions

Dreams become powerful when translated into clear intentions. This step mirrors Jedi training, where mastery is built on deliberate practice.

Provide a framework for inmates to outline their intentions:

1. **Identify Specific Goals** – Define short- and long-term aspirations (e.g., improving communication skills, completing education).

2. **Connect to Emotions** – Reflect on what achieving these goals would *feel* like. Emotional connection strengthens resilience.

3. **Create an Action Plan** – Break each goal into practical, manageable steps. Just as Jedi train tirelessly before wielding a lightsaber, inmates must design roadmaps to guide their journey.

Exercise 5: Reflection Journal

Introduce journaling as an ongoing practice to reinforce commitment.

Prompts might include:

- *What progress have I made toward my goals this week?*

- *What challenges have I faced, and how did I respond?*

- *What have I learned about myself in this process?*

- *How has my vision evolved since I began?*

Over time, the journal becomes a chronicle of resilience and growth a testament to transformation.

Exercise 6: Visualization Techniques

Finally, teach inmates to practice **visualization** a technique Jedi use in honing their skills.

- Guide participants to close their eyes and vividly imagine achieving their goals.

- Encourage them to picture the details: What does success look like? How does it feel? How do others respond?

- Reinforce the idea that this exercise can be revisited whenever motivation wanes.

Through visualization, aspirations shift from abstract ideas to lived experiences rehearsed in the mind.

Creating an Environment for Vision Crafting

For vision crafting to thrive, the institution itself must foster an environment that sustains hope:

1. **Support Groups** – Regular gatherings where inmates share progress, victories, and challenges.

2. **Mentorship Programs** – Pairing inmates with mentors or volunteers who guide them on their journey.

3. **Integration of Arts and Education** – Offering creative outlets and skill-based programs aligned with vision-building.

4. **Access to Resources** – Providing books, films, and counseling that reinforce themes of resilience and hope.

5. **Celebrating Success** – Recognizing milestones, big or small, reinforces motivation and belief in change.

Kicking Off Their Lightsabers

Vision crafting is not idle daydreaming it is a practice that ignites dormant fire within the soul. By reflecting, dreaming, and setting intentions, inmates learn to navigate life with renewed clarity and purpose.

Like Jedi apprentices facing trials, inmates will encounter setbacks. Yet each challenge becomes a teacher. Resilience, courage, and the commitment to growth are the true forces that guide them toward transformation.

Vision crafting ultimately reminds individuals that the journey itself is as important as the destination. Each step forward no matter how small enriches the spirit and strengthens resolve. With lightsabers ignited in the metaphorical sense, inmates can step into the galaxy of their futures, ready to shine brightly with purpose and hope.

Support Systems for Hope

Support systems are vital for anyone striving to cultivate hope, but for inmates, they can mean the difference between despair and the possibility of a brighter future. In many ways, the concept of community mirrors the teachings of the Jedi. The Jedi Order was built upon relationships, fostering a collective strength that could endure even the darkest times.

This subchapter explores the importance of surrounding oneself with a supportive community, drawing on Jedi wisdom and practical strategies for inmates to build networks of hope and to become beacons of hope for one another.

Hope as a Shared Experience

The Jedi understood that hope is not solely an individual pursuit but a shared experience, illuminated by communal bonds. In the same way, inmates can find strength in their connections with one another. Each person brings unique struggles and triumphs, and together they form a mosaic of resilience.

Finding hope in darkness requires cultivating relationships grounded in empathy, understanding, and encouragement. The first step is deceptively simple: **being present for one another.**

Jedi are trained to be attuned to the emotions and needs of others. Inmates, too, can practice this awareness listening deeply, sharing stories, and creating safe spaces for dialogue. The act of truly listening validates experiences and fosters meaningful connections.

Mentorship: A Jedi Tradition

Mentorship is another pillar of Jedi philosophy. Just as Padawans learn from their Masters, inmates can establish mentoring relationships that benefit both parties.

- **Mentors**: Inmates with longer sentences or more experience can guide those new to prison life, offering coping strategies and encouragement.

- **Mentees**: Those receiving guidance gain insight, support, and reassurance in navigating challenges.

For mentors, the role itself fosters purpose and fulfillment. They become part of a legacy of support, nurturing hope in others while reinforcing their own identities.

Reaching Beyond the Walls

Support systems need not stop at prison gates. Connections with family, friends, or community groups focused on rehabilitation can serve as lifelines.

- Letters from loved ones provide encouragement and continuity.

- Educational or volunteer programs create a sense of belonging to something larger than oneself.

- Community mentors can inspire hope for reintegration and success after release.

These external ties remind inmates that their lives extend beyond confinement and that they remain part of a broader, supportive network.

Building Community Within

Support networks can also flourish inside correctional facilities. Inmates can form **study groups, discussion circles, or hobby clubs** that promote personal development and collective healing. Much like the Jedi Council gathered to deliberate, these groups provide structure for meaningful dialogue and growth.

Topics may range from emotional well-being to skill-building, but the essential element is the bond created through shared experiences.

Giving Hope Through Action

Fostering hope is not only about receiving support it is also about giving it.

Inmates can embody Jedi-like compassion by:

- Leading peer counseling sessions.

- Organizing community events.

- Offering daily encouragement to others.

They may also channel emotions through **creative outlets** such as art, writing, or performance. Just as Jedi use the Force as a conduit for expression, inmates can turn their experiences into works of beauty and inspiration. Creative expression not only provides therapy but also sparks hope in those who witness it.

Celebrating Success

Another way to strengthen hope is by celebrating success stories. Highlighting individual victories no matter how small uplifts the entire group.

Recognizing transformations demonstrates that change is possible, reinforcing the belief that growth and healing are within reach. This practice encourages a culture of encouragement, accountability, and pride in progress.

Diversity and Unity

The Jedi Order thrived on diversity, valuing the unique strengths of each member. In the same way, inmate support systems should embrace diversity. Each person's story contributes valuable perspective, deepening collective understanding.

Respecting differences and finding unity in shared humanity fosters resilience and a sense of belonging.

Building a Culture of Trust

Support systems require a foundation of respect, trust, and non-judgment. Establishing ground rules such as confidentiality and mutual respect creates safety for vulnerability. When inmates feel free to share openly, authentic bonds can form.

Establishing support systems is fundamental to nurturing hope, just as communal ties sustained the Jedi. By embracing presence, mentorship, external connections, group activities, creativity, and celebration, inmates can build networks that illuminate the path toward healing and transformation.

Such systems not only sustain individual hope but also inspire members to contribute actively to the collective mission of resilience. Through shared effort, an atmosphere of compassion and understanding emerges empowering each person to rise to their potential and share that light with others.

Just as the Force binds the galaxy, so too can hope bind a community. The journey toward healing need not be undertaken in isolation; it thrives in solidarity, teamwork, and compassion. By embodying these principles, inmates can foster hope in their own lives and ignite it in the lives of others.

Chapter 7: Resilience: The Foundation of a Jedi

Building Mental Resilience

Resilience is often spoken of in hushed tones, as though it were a mystical gift reserved for a chosen few. Yet resilience is not unattainable it is not a gift but a skill, one that can be nurtured and honed over time, much like the elegance of a carefully wielded lightsaber. Within the confines of incarceration, resilience becomes essential. These walls, built to confine and control, often mirror the internal struggles inmates confront daily.

The Jedi, as portrayed in the Star Wars universe, embody a remarkable capacity for resilience in the face of overwhelming challenges. In this exploration, we will weave together fictional lessons from the Jedi and real-life stories of transformation, while providing actionable practices that inmates can adopt to cultivate emotional fortitude.

Resilience in the Jedi Path

To understand resilience, consider the life of a Jedi. They are not infallible they encounter failure, loss, and profound doubt. What distinguishes them is not freedom from adversity but their unwavering capacity to rise again.

Take Anakin Skywalker, for instance. His journey is scarred by ambition, trauma, and eventual downfall into Darth Vader. Yet even in his darkest moments, flashes of resilience emerged, often fueled by his love for others. His inner conflict reminds us that resilience is not defined by perfection but by the willingness to reflect, learn, and rise again despite our flaws.

Inmates face their own battles uncertainty, loss of freedom, rejection, and diminished self-worth. These struggles can weaken the spirit. But resilience is not an abstract notion; it is grounded in human experience. It grows from recognizing one's strengths in the midst of adversity and from accepting the support of others.

Sometimes, resilience is found in small acts: a fellow inmate patiently listening during a moment of despair, or a peer offering encouragement rather than judgment. These simple gestures echo the Jedi principle of community and interdependence. Just as Jedi draw strength from one another, inmates too can build resilience by fostering supportive bonds.

Practices for Cultivating Resilience

Resilience is not passive it must be practiced. Here are some pathways to strengthen it:

1. **Adopt a Growth Mindset**: Resilience begins with perspective. A growth mindset the belief that abilities and intelligence can be developed through effort is foundational. Inmates can choose to see their time not only as punishment but as an opportunity to learn. Each day offers lessons, whether through education, mentorship, or self-study.

2. **Journaling for Reflection**: Writing can be a powerful act of resilience. Putting pen to paper allows inmates to process emotions, confront fears, celebrate victories, and clarify goals. In this way, journaling mirrors Jedi meditation reflection as a path to wisdom. By reclaiming their stories, inmates can transform their past into a source of strength instead of shame.

3. **Physical Activity**: The mind and body are deeply connected. Exercise reduces anxiety and depression while strengthening resilience. Whether through sports, martial arts, or daily walks, physical training parallels Jedi discipline. Just as the Jedi sharpen their bodies to sharpen their minds, inmates can build emotional fortitude through physical endurance.

4. **Mindfulness and Meditation**: In turbulent environments, inner calm is rare but vital. Guided meditation, deep breathing, and mindfulness exercises help inmates stay present, manage stress, and cultivate clarity. Just as Jedi connect with the Force to center themselves, inmates can connect with their breath and awareness to find grounding strength.

5. **Peer Support**: Collective resilience magnifies individual strength. Support groups, shared stories, and group goals create belonging and validation. When sorrows and joys are shared, resilience blossoms in fellowship, proving that no one has to walk their journey alone.

6. **Gratitude Practice**: Gratitude transforms outlooks. The Jedi embody appreciation for even the smallest moments of joy. Inmates can cultivate resilience by reflecting daily on three things they are grateful for, no matter how small. Gratitude shifts focus from despair to possibility.

7. **Visualization**: Jedi often visualize the peace they fight for. Inmates can use visualization to imagine rebuilding their lives, reconnecting with loved ones, or achieving dreams. This practice strengthens belief in a brighter future and motivates action toward it.

A Story of Resilience

In one correctional facility, a young woman named Sarah struggled under the weight of regret, convinced her life was chained to past mistakes. Yet through a rehabilitation program that emphasized growth, she found purpose. Encouraged by peers and counselors, she began teaching basic literacy to other inmates.

In that act of service, Sarah mirrored a Jedi's journey not just learning, but uplifting others with her knowledge. In doing so, she discovered compassion for herself and for those around her. Her resilience deepened, leading her to self-forgiveness and hope for the future.

Her story reminds us that resilience often emerges from vulnerability. By transforming her pain into purpose, Sarah built a foundation of strength not only for herself but for those she helped.

The Role of Purpose and Patience

Resilience grows stronger when anchored in purpose. Jedi are guided by their commitment to the Light Side, giving them strength to endure trials. Inmates too can identify their own guiding purpose family, reconciliation, education, or service. Clear, meaningful goals transform adversity into steppingstones toward healing.

Patience is equally crucial. The Jedi path takes years of training, marked by setbacks as well as triumphs. Inmates must also understand that resilience develops gradually. Emotional growth is not linear failures will happen. What matters is the commitment to continue rising, step after step.

In the grand tapestry of life, resilience is the thread that binds moments of hardship to moments of triumph. The Jedi exemplify this, embodying clarity of purpose and the resolve to rise even after defeat.

Resilience is not innate it is cultivated. Like a Jedi mastering the lightsaber, inmates can train themselves in resilience through community, mindfulness, physical discipline, gratitude, and purpose. Each practice strengthens the spirit and transforms confinement into a training ground for growth.

Ultimately, building mental resilience is not about mere survival it is about thriving in the face of adversity. Just as the Jedi face the trials of the galaxy, inmates too can rise, transforming their struggles into legacies of perseverance, hope, and strength.

Stories of Resilience

In the vast expanse of human experience, stories of resilience shine like stars in the night sky. Each tale of adversity faced and overcome encapsulates the essence of perseverance: the drive to rise from darkness and find a path to the light. This subchapter explores several inspiring narratives of individuals who transformed their lives, echoing the noble tenets of Jedi wisdom. Their journeys offer not only motivation but also structured lessons for inmates seeking to confront their own challenges.

Marcus: Choosing Hope

Consider the story of Marcus, a young man whose life was enveloped in despair. Growing up in a neighborhood rife with crime and limited opportunities, he felt trapped in a cycle that seemed impossible to escape. By his teenage years, he had succumbed to that environment, making choices that eventually led to incarceration.

In prison, the weight of regret bore heavily on him. At times, hopelessness threatened to engulf him. Yet within those walls, Marcus began his journey toward resilience. Inspired by childhood tales of heroes who overcame impossible odds, he drew strength from the Jedi principle of hope. Determined not to let his circumstances define him, Marcus chose to confront his struggles directly.

He engaged in therapy, facing the feelings he had long buried. Each session became a step along his own path with the Force, teaching him not only to face his fears but to understand them. He saw parallels with Anakin Skywalker, whose own fall into darkness was tempered by moments of clarity. Like Anakin, Marcus learned that resilience is not about avoiding pain but transforming it into strength.

Over time, Marcus devoted himself to education, studying philosophy, conflict resolution, and psychology. He dreamed of becoming a counselor who could help others navigate their dark paths. With each lesson, he fortified his resilience, reminding himself of the Jedi Code and of the redemption possible in every life.

Elena: Rebuilding Through Connection

Another powerful example of resilience is Elena, a woman whose journey resonates with many who face systemic challenges. She grew up in chaos and was eventually trapped in cycles of substance abuse. Multiple rehabilitation attempts left her disheartened, each failure convincing her that recovery was slipping further away.

Her breakthrough came unexpectedly during a group therapy session. As she shared her story with others, she realized that strength could be found in community. The Jedi doctrine emphasizes connection and the wisdom of shared struggle, and Elena embraced this. She discovered she was not alone and that her experiences could help guide others.

With encouragement from her peers, Elena committed herself to discipline and mindfulness, adopting practices much like those taught in the Jedi Temple. Through meditation and structure, she gradually harnessed her thoughts, resisting the temptations that had once consumed her. Resilience began to blossom.

She completed rehabilitation and later became a motivational speaker, sharing her story with those still struggling with addiction. Her journey mirrored that of Ahsoka Tano, who, though she left the Jedi Order, found renewed purpose and emerged wiser and stronger. Elena, too, reclaimed her identity and transformed her past into a beacon of hope. Her life stands as proof that amidst chaos, resilience can illuminate the way forward.

Ian: From Regret to Service

The story of Ian further illustrates resilience in action. Incarcerated for several years after an impulsive crime, he was haunted by the pain his actions had caused not only to himself but to others. The darkness of his past weighed heavily on him, yet rather than giving in to despair, Ian chose to confront his mistakes head-on, much like Luke Skywalker facing his fate.

Through group therapy, he learned to articulate his feelings and take ownership of his actions. Inspired by the Jedi value of self-awareness, Ian came to understand the ripple effects of his choices. With this reflection came compassion and a deeper sense of justice.

He began volunteering within the prison, supporting other inmates who struggled with despair. His service echoed the Jedi's commitment to helping others in times of need. By embodying empathy and responsibility, Ian not only found healing for himself but became a source of inspiration for those around him. His resilience was forged through accountability, compassion, and service.

Maria: Healing Through Acceptance

The triumph of resilience is beautifully embodied in the story of Maria, who faced chronic mental health struggles intensified by the harshness of her environment. Her childhood was marked by trauma and instability, and by the time she entered the prison system, she already felt like a lost soul. Like many of her peers, Maria wrestled with isolation, hopelessness, and despair conflicts akin to the emotional battles faced by Jedi grappling with doubt and fear.

Her pivotal moment came when she discovered the practices of mindfulness and the importance of caring for her mental health. Through journaling and participation in therapeutic communities, Maria began to give voice to her story, transforming her pain into something meaningful. This act of expression not only provided her with solace but also opened the door to connection with others.

Maria saw her journey reflected in the struggles of Jedi who faced their own darkness yet emerged with deeper wisdom and renewed purpose. She came to understand resilience through the lens of self-kindness, embodying the Jedi principle of acceptance without judgment. By embracing acceptance, she reframed her struggles not as permanent flaws but as experiences that enriched her understanding of both strength and vulnerability.

This newfound insight allowed Maria to heal and, just as importantly, to extend that healing outward. She became a mentor to fellow inmates, guiding them through their own labyrinths of confusion and despair. In doing so, she transformed her own suffering into a beacon of light for others.

The Collective Lesson of Resilience

The stories of Marcus, Elena, Ian, and Maria serve as profound reminders of the potential for transformation within every individual. Together, they embody the heart of the Jedi ethos: even in the shadows, there always lies the possibility of light.

For inmates, understanding that they are not alone in their struggles and that change is not only possible but achievable can provide the courage to take those first, daunting steps toward a new life. Each narrative highlights a guiding principle of resilience:

- **Hope**, as Marcus discovered in his commitment to growth.

- **Community**, as Elena found in her support networks.

- **Self-awareness**, as Ian embraced in his accountability and service.

- **Acceptance**, as Maria embodied through mindfulness and mentorship.

These lessons reveal that struggle does not equate to failure; rather, it can become the very catalyst for growth. By embracing Jedi teachings alongside their own unique stories, inmates can cultivate resilience, emerging from hardship equipped with wisdom, compassion, and strength.

In a world that often feels overwhelming, these narratives offer powerful tools for healing and rebirth. They remind us that adversity can shape not shatter the human spirit, guiding each individual closer to their true self. Just as the Jedi harness the Force to fulfill their destiny, inmates too can rise from the shadows, transformed into beacons of hope and resilience.

Practicing Resilience Daily

To cultivate resilience akin to that of a Jedi, it is essential to integrate specific exercises and practices into daily life. This subchapter aims to provide practical guidance for building resilience, drawing on the wisdom of Jedi philosophies while intertwining it with actionable strategies. Resilience is not merely an innate trait; it is a skill that can be developed and strengthened over time through consistent practice and mindfulness.

The journey toward resilience begins with a mindset that embraces challenges as opportunities for growth. It requires an understanding that each obstacle faced can serve as a stepping stone, leading to transformation both internally and externally. The path of the Jedi teaches us that perseverance is the cornerstone of the light side of the Force, and this principle can guide us as we foster resilience in ourselves and in our environments.

One of the first practices that can lead to increased resilience is the cultivation of mindfulness. Mindfulness encourages individuals to engage fully with the present moment, creating a space in their

91

minds for reflection, clarity, and calmness. This practice is essential, especially for those facing the unique challenges of incarceration. By focusing on the present, one can observe thoughts and feelings without judgment, allowing for a better understanding of emotional responses in difficult situations.

A simple exercise to cultivate mindfulness is the **"Five Senses Exercise."** Set aside just a few minutes each day to engage with your surroundings using your five senses. Find a quiet place where you can sit comfortably. Take a few deep breaths, letting your body relax. Begin by noting five things you can see around you. Then identify four things you can feel, three things you hear, two things you can smell, and finally, one thing you can taste. This practice not only grounds you in the present moment but also enhances your awareness of the environment, helping you recognize that even in challenging times, there are small joys to be savored.

In addition to mindfulness, establishing a daily gratitude practice can significantly bolster resilience. Gratitude shifts focus from what is lacking to recognizing the positive elements that exist in one's life, even in difficult circumstances. A gratitude journal can be an effective tool in this process. Each day, spend a few moments reflecting on three things you are grateful for, no matter how small. This could range from appreciating a moment of warmth from the sun or the support of fellow inmates, to the simple pleasure of reading a good book. Over time, this practice reframes the mind to recognize abundance rather than scarcity. It emphasizes that even amidst chaos or uncertainty, there are still aspects of life that can bring joy and contentment. This Jedi-like appreciation for life aligns with the belief that every moment holds potential for learning and growth.

Embracing challenges also requires a proactive attitude an essential principle of the Jedi way. Each individual's journey through incarceration is unique, but facing challenges head-on transforms them from barriers into opportunities. One effective daily practice to encourage this mindset is to identify and confront one small fear or challenge each day. This could mean having a difficult conversation with a fellow inmate, participating in an unfamiliar group activity, or even voicing your opinions more freely. Start by writing down a list of fears or challenges that feel present in your life. Then select one to focus on each day. Allow yourself to fully feel the apprehension, but commit to taking a step forward regardless. Observe the outcome, reflect on the experience, and recognize the strength gained from that confrontation. By engaging with fear instead of avoiding it, individuals cultivate a warrior's spirit essential for true resilience.

Another discipline drawn from Jedi teachings is the importance of self-discipline and routine. Establishing a daily structure can aid in managing thoughts and feelings, especially in the unpredictable environment of incarceration. A well-defined daily routine can provide a sense of normalcy and control, elements that are often stripped away in such settings. Create a daily schedule that includes time for personal reflection, physical activity, education, and social engagement. Designate specific time blocks for each activity to ensure balance. For instance, begin the day with a morning reflection practice followed by physical exercise, perhaps by engaging in yoga or basic workouts. Afterward, allocate time for reading or pursuing educational opportunities, and finally, set aside moments for socializing with fellow inmates. This structured approach embodies the Jedi principle that a balanced life leads to a clearer mind and a stronger spirit.

Physical exercise, specifically, is a powerful component of building resilience. The Jedi understood the value of physical fitness as not only a means to prepare for battle but also as a way to maintain mental clarity and emotional equilibrium. Regular physical activity releases endorphins, often referred to as "feel-good" hormones, which can combat feelings of anxiety and depression prevalent in incarceration. Incorporate physical activities such as walking, running, or participating in group sports into your daily routine. Even simple exercises like calisthenics or stretching can make a significant difference in overall well-being. Additionally, consider practicing disciplines like martial arts or tai chi, which not only improve physical fitness but also emphasize discipline, respect, and self-control qualities that resonate deeply with the Jedi way.

Another method to foster resilience is the practice of visualization. Visualization is a powerful mental exercise that involves picturing oneself overcoming obstacles or achieving goals. This technique not only bolsters confidence but also prepares the mind to face real-life challenges with greater assurance. Set aside a few minutes each day to visualize your desired outcomes or envision yourself navigating through challenges successfully. Imagine how it feels to overcome adversity, and allow that emotional resonance to infuse your actions and thoughts.

Incorporating the teachings of Jedi philosophy, it is vital to channel the Force within oneself for guidance and resilience. Meditative practices, such as focused breathing, can anchor you during tumultuous times. Take a moment each day to practice controlled breathing: inhale for a count of four, hold for a count of four, and exhale for a count of four. Repeat this cycle for a few minutes, allowing each breath to cleanse the mind of negativity and fill it with clarity and peace.

Jedi wisdom also emphasizes the importance of community and connection, which are essential factors in building resilience. Having a support system provides encouragement, strength, and alternative perspectives during challenging times. Foster connections with others wherever possible, whether through dialogue, shared activities, or group reflections. Engage in meaningful conversations that cultivate understanding and foster compassion. The light side of the Force strengthens when individuals unite and support each other.

In addition to external support, self-compassion is crucial for resilience. Jedi teachings advocate for treating oneself with kindness, especially in times of struggle. Often, inner dialogue can be harsh or critical, emphasizing feelings of failure or inadequacy.

Acknowledge these feelings without judgment and practice self-compassion. Speak to yourself as you would to a friend encourage, uplift, and affirm your worth. This approach allows for greater emotional resilience, as it fosters acceptance in the face of difficulty.

Finally, consider engaging in creative expression as a means to process emotions and experiences. Creativity whether through writing, art, music, or other forms can be a powerful outlet for feelings that may otherwise overwhelm. Setting aside time each day to engage in a creative practice invites vulnerability and exploration of emotions, ultimately leading to greater self-awareness and resilience. Allow your creativity to be a bridge to understanding your experiences and a reminder of the latent strength within you.

As we weave these daily practices into our lives, it becomes increasingly apparent that resilience is not merely about enduring hardship; it is about transforming ourselves through it. Each small action taken toward cultivating resilience can ultimately lead to profound transformation. Just as Jedi face the trials of the Dark Side, we too can confront our difficulties with courage, tenacity, and grace. Through consistent practice of these exercises, we harness the energy of the Force, empowering ourselves to rise stronger each day.

In conclusion, as we embrace the teachings of Jedi wisdom, we must remember that resilience is a journey, not a destination. The path may be fraught with challenges, yet it is in the active practice of resilience that we find growth and transformation. By fostering mindfulness, gratitude, confrontation of fears, structured routines, physical fitness, visualization, community connection, self-compassion, and creativity, we build the foundation needed to withstand life's adversities.

As we step forth into each new day, empowered by these practices, we become the architects of our resilience. Let the journey of a Jedi inspire us, reminding us that resilience is not only essential for survival but also a channel for thriving and flourishing through the challenges we encounter, forging our way with the unwavering spirit of growth and perseverance that defines a true Jedi.

Chapter 8: The Inner Jedi: Awakening Strength

Identifying Inner Strengths

In the grand tapestry of Jedi philosophy, woven through the teachings of the Force and the principles of self-discovery, lies a profound understanding of one's own inner strengths. Within the confines of a prison, where the shadows of doubt and despair can often overshadow the light of hope, rediscovering these strengths can be a powerful tool for healing and transformation. This journey not only connects inmates to their personal growth but also resonates deeply with the Jedi teachings of self-acceptance and inner balance.

The process of identifying inner strengths begins with an essential premise: each individual carries within them a unique set of abilities, qualities, and attributes that can serve as tools for resilience and empowerment. Just as a Jedi learns to harness the Force, individuals must explore their own strengths to navigate the challenges they face. The act of self-discovery is not merely an introspective endeavor; it is an exercise in embracing one's true self an awakening of the hidden potential within.

To embark on this journey of self-discovery, we will engage in a series of reflective exercises and guided questions. These will not only guide the reader through the nuances of their experiences but also provide clarity on the strengths they possess. Participants are encouraged to find a quiet space, free from distractions, where they can thoughtfully engage with these questions. Journaling responses will help to capture insights and track growth.

Reflecting on Past Challenges

As the first step, consider a moment in your life when you faced a significant challenge. Reflect on how you responded to that situation. Was there a specific quality or strength that emerged during this time? Perhaps it was determination that carried you forward, or compassion that motivated you to reach out to others. Write down this experience and the strengths that surfaced. The act of recognizing these traits can be eye-opening; they are often most visible in hindsight.

Next, delve deeper into how these strengths contributed to overcoming the challenge. Did your empathy help you find support? Did resilience inspire you to push through the hardest moments? This analysis is not meant to paint a perfect picture, but rather to shed light on the many dimensions of strength that arise in times of struggle. Each quality identified is a facet of your inner Jedi, echoing the teachings of self-acceptance and growth.

Exploring Current Strengths

With past challenges in mind, turn to the present. What qualities do you appreciate most about yourself today? Perhaps courage is what you admire the bold step of engaging with this material despite your circumstances. Maybe it's creativity, the ability to envision a brighter future beyond your environment. Write down three to five qualities that resonate with you now. These attributes serve as the foundation for resilience and personal development.

The Power of Feedback

Next, practice the art of feedback. Reach out to someone you trust a fellow inmate, a mentor, or a family member and ask them to share what they consider your strengths. Often, others can see qualities within us that we overlook. Their perspectives can validate your self-image or reveal strengths you had not yet recognized. By embracing their insights, you expand your understanding of self, aligning with the Jedi principle of community and connection.

Applying Strengths in Daily Life

Now, consider how these strengths shape your daily life, both inside and outside the prison walls. For instance, how has your ability to remain calm in stressful situations helped you navigate conflicts? How has empathy allowed you to build supportive connections? Documenting these instances reinforces the knowledge that your strengths are not only present but actively contributing to your journey.

Confronting Doubt

As you explore your strengths, doubts may arise. Like the Sith who succumb to despair, we can easily become trapped in negativity. Write down any critical thoughts that surface, such as *"I'm not good enough"* or *"I don't have any strengths."* Acknowledging these thoughts is the first step. Then, challenge them. For each negative belief, write a counter-statement that affirms your strengths. For example: *"I may struggle at times, but I have valuable qualities that can guide me."* Recognizing and reframing these thoughts is akin to Jedi training transforming fear into courage.

Strengths for the Greater Good

Balance is at the heart of Jedi wisdom, and it is important to see how strengths extend beyond oneself. In what ways can you use your qualities to enhance the lives of others? Perhaps your ability to motivate can inspire a peer to pursue growth, or your talent for listening can provide support to someone in pain. Documenting these realizations reinforces the interconnectedness of individuals and the shared potential for positive change.

Embracing Complexity

Jedi teachings emphasize self-acceptance and remind us that every strength can be a gift. Embrace the complexity of your traits; they need not fit neatly into one category. Your assertiveness may help you advocate for yourself, while your kindness fosters meaningful relationships. Recognizing these nuances promotes deeper self-awareness and appreciation.

Peak Experiences and Visualization

Reflect on moments when you felt entirely in tune with your strengths. What were you doing? Who were you with? These peak experiences are signposts of your potential, showing where your strengths shine brightest.

Next, visualize your future. Where do you see yourself in five years? What qualities do you want to embody? What strengths do you wish to cultivate further? By envisioning your future self, you not only set intentions but also highlight which strengths to nurture. Write down these intentions and commit to small, steady steps toward them.

Gratitude and Ongoing Practice

Practice intentional gratitude for your strengths. Dedicate a few minutes each day to reflect on specific qualities and give thanks for them. Gratitude deepens appreciation, reinforces self-acceptance, and strengthens resilience.

Remember: discovering and embracing inner strengths is an ongoing journey. Just as Jedi continually train, so must you prioritize self-exploration. Revisit these exercises regularly, recognizing that growth is not linear. Some days, you may feel empowered; on others, doubt may creep in. Hold space for both. True strength is found in embracing the full spectrum of experience.

Ultimately, recognizing your inner strengths is not merely an act of acknowledgment; it is a commitment to move forward with openness and courage. By aligning self-understanding with Jedi wisdom, you foster resilience and empowerment.

As you conclude this exploration, review the qualities you've identified. Circle the three or four that resonate most strongly. These are your guiding stars the strengths that will illuminate your path as you walk in the light of the Force. Embrace them, nurture them, and let them become the foundation of your journey toward transformation and healing.

Celebrate your strengths as the lightsabers of your inner Jedi powerful tools to navigate darkness and carve a path toward hope, connection, and empowerment. By uncovering and embracing these qualities, you honor the Jedi way and step boldly into a future filled with possibility. Your self-discovery not only reinforces resilience but contributes to the broader narrative of healing and growth within the community. In doing so, you fulfill the promise of the Jedi: to bring balance to the Force, within yourself and among others.

Building Self-Confidence

Building self-confidence is an essential aspect of personal development, particularly for individuals in challenging circumstances such as those in correctional facilities. In the context of this book, we draw a unique correlation between self-esteem and the qualities of a Jedi a symbol of inner strength, discipline, and resilience. *Star Wars* lore provides valuable insights into self-discovery and empowerment, which can resonate deeply with inmates striving to find their path amid adversity. This subchapter will explore various techniques for building self-confidence while encouraging inmates to embody their strengths and take ownership of their narratives.

To cultivate self-confidence, it is critical to first understand the traits associated with a Jedi. Jedi possess unwavering belief in themselves, a deep understanding of their abilities, and a commitment to personal growth. They embody virtues such as courage, patience, and compassion, which empower them not only to face challenges but to uplift others as well. By paralleling these traits with practical techniques, we can guide inmates to awaken their inner Jedi and tap into their potential.

One of the most effective ways to build self-confidence is through **positive self-talk**. The dialogue we maintain with ourselves significantly influences our perception of our capabilities. Inmates often face societal stigmas and internalized negative beliefs that can undermine their self-worth. Encouraging them to practice positive affirmations can be a transformative exercise. Begin by inviting them to write down three qualities they appreciate in themselves. These can range from traits such as flexibility or determination to skills like resourcefulness or communication. Once identified, guide them to articulate these qualities into affirmations. For example: *"I am resourceful and can overcome challenges,"* or *"My determination helps me achieve my goals."* Encourage inmates to recite these affirmations daily, preferably in front of a mirror, to reinforce a positive self-image. The act of voicing their strengths serves as a powerful reminder of their potential, much like a Jedi reaffirming their connection with the Force.

Another practical exercise involves **setting small, achievable goals**, which can be pivotal in incrementally building self-confidence. Goals act as markers of progress, and with each success, an individual's belief in their abilities is reinforced. Inmates can start by identifying something they want to improve or change, such as enhancing literacy skills, developing a hobby, or engaging in physical fitness. Break these goals into manageable steps. For instance, if the objective is to read a book, the initial step could be to read one chapter per week. Every time a step is achieved, inmates should take a moment to celebrate their success, no matter how small. These small victories are essential, reinforcing the idea that they are capable of growth and change.

In addition to goal setting, understanding the **journey of mastering skills** can bolster self-confidence. Jedi training emphasizes practice and perseverance, embodying the mantra *"failure is a teacher."* Encourage inmates to view setbacks as learning experiences rather than as indicators of worth. For example, in a group setting, they could discuss challenges they've faced and how they overcame them. Such discussions can inspire others to reframe their perceptions of failure.

Similarly, fostering a **growth mindset** can significantly impact self-esteem. Coined by psychologist Carol Dweck, this concept posits that abilities and intelligence can be developed through dedication and hard work. Teaching inmates the difference between a fixed mindset (which limits potential) and a growth mindset (which nurtures it) can be transformative. Help them understand that their past does not define their future they have the power to change their story. Exercises might include brainstorming sessions where inmates identify passions and interests, or reflecting on moments when they felt proud or successfully learned something new. These reflections create a roadmap toward adopting a growth mindset.

Mindfulness practices also play an essential role in building self-confidence. Jedi teachings emphasize presence and awareness, which can help individuals manage emotions and reduce anxiety. Encourage inmates to practice mindfulness exercises such as deep breathing or meditation to connect with their inner selves. Simple guided meditations focusing on self-acceptance and self-love can be powerful tools for cultivating a positive mindset. For instance, inmates can visualize themselves overcoming challenges while embodying Jedi traits. Imagining themselves standing strong, making wise decisions, or showing compassion reinforces the reality that these qualities already exist within them. Reinforce the importance of making these sessions routine, just as Jedi commit to ongoing training and self-improvement.

Social support and collaboration are also critical components of self-confidence. Create group activities that encourage inmates to share their strengths, goals, and struggles. This can be done through workshops or study groups where constructive dialogue thrives. Sharing experiences fosters community and helps individuals see that others share similar challenges and triumphs. Encouraging inmates to act as mentors or facilitators for their peers can further solidify their self-esteem. Teaching others reinforces one's own knowledge and capabilities. Team-building exercises where they guide discussions, share skills, or lead activities embody the Jedi principle of service and strengthen belief in personal worth.

Another powerful technique is **visualization**. Jedi often visualize their goals, training their focus and intention. Encourage inmates to employ visualization techniques aligned with their aspirations. They can imagine themselves in the future having achieved their goals and visualize the steps taken to get there. This mental imagery enhances motivation and affirms their belief in their abilities to manifest outcomes.

In addition, **journaling** can serve as a therapeutic tool for inmates to articulate thoughts and reflect on experiences. Encourage them to keep a personal journal to record feelings, aspirations, and daily achievements. Journaling promotes self-reflection and allows individuals to externalize their thoughts, leading to greater clarity and understanding. Dedicate part of the practice to reflecting on moments of bravery or strength such as standing up for themselves, making difficult decisions, or helping a peer. By documenting these instances, inmates build a narrative of resilience that reiterates their capabilities and worth.

Ultimately, fostering an environment of encouragement, support, and positivity is fundamental to nurturing self-confidence among inmates. Create programs that promote personal development through workshops, discussions, and collaborative projects. Facilitate activities that highlight Jedi qualities such as teamwork, discipline, and compassion. Empowering inmates to embody the qualities of a Jedi and recognize their strengths is transformative.

By integrating these strategies into daily routines, inmates can gradually shift their self-perception and narrative. Through self-acceptance, goal setting, a growth mindset, mindfulness, and social connection, they can build the self-esteem necessary to navigate challenges with the courage and determination that Jedi exhibit.

In sum, building self-confidence is an ongoing journey requiring commitment and practice, much like the Jedi commitment to training in the ways of the Force. By providing inmates with practical techniques and encouraging them to embody their strengths, we create a pathway toward empowerment and self-discovery. They must remember that the Force resides within them, waiting to be awakened. Through nurturing their self-confidence, inmates not only change their own narratives but also inspire those around them by demonstrating what is possible when one believes in oneself.

Accountability and Growth

The journey of personal growth is one marked by commitment, self-awareness, and a dedication to meaningful change. For those within the walls of correctional facilities, the potential for transformation may seem distant, overshadowed by the weight of past decisions and the conditions of confinement. However, as with the teachings of the Jedi, strength can be found in accountability and community. This subchapter focuses on how embracing accountability fosters growth, echoing the transformative paths taken by those who train to become Jedi.

Accountability is a cornerstone of Jedi philosophy. Jedi are taught to understand themselves, their actions, and the implications those actions have on their path and on the lives of others. They take ownership of their decisions, learning from every mistake and triumph. This practice is not unique to the Jedi; it is a universal principle that can guide personal transformation. By understanding the importance of accountability, inmates can shift their perspectives, recognizing that every challenge presents an opportunity for growth.

Establishing accountability begins with honest self-reflection. In the *Star Wars* universe, Jedi often meditate, seeking clarity and insight into their thoughts and actions. In a similar way, inmates are encouraged to engage in their own form of introspection. A daily journaling practice is one effective method. Through writing, individuals can track their thoughts, emotions, and patterns of behavior, fostering a deeper understanding of themselves. This doesn't need to be complex even simple entries reflecting on the day's activities, choices, and feelings can pave the way for greater self-awareness.

To cultivate accountability, it is essential to set clear, achievable goals. Just as a Jedi sets out to master the ways of the Force, individuals in correctional settings can define their own aspirations for personal growth. These goals may range from rebuilding relationships with family, to acquiring new skills, or developing emotional regulation techniques. Each goal should incorporate measurable steps that can be documented over time. Breaking down larger aspirations into smaller milestones creates a roadmap that leads toward eventual success.

Engaging with others fosters an environment of shared accountability and mutual support. The Jedi Order is built upon collaboration and mentorship, where members uplift each other throughout their journeys. Inmates can benefit equally from forming accountability groups within prison. These groups can provide a safe space to share goals, challenges, and successes. Regular check-ins encourage members to hold each other to their commitments, creating a culture of trust and camaraderie.

In these accountability groups, members may engage in activities that reinforce their resolve to grow. One exercise could involve creating a **vision board** a visual representation of aspirations. Members can cut out images and phrases from magazines that resonate with their goals, displaying their boards in a shared space. This visual aspect serves as a constant reminder, instilling motivation to pursue their path with determination.

Another vital exercise is sharing **personal stories of failure and redemption**. In the Jedi tradition, immense value is placed on learning from mistakes. By speaking openly about past errors, inmates can shed the stigma of guilt that often accompanies incarceration. These discussions foster connection, allowing members to realize they are not alone in their struggles. Sharing experiences also promotes growth, as individuals learn coping strategies and insights from one another's journeys.

Accountability can sometimes bring discomfort, particularly when it involves confronting difficult truths. Like Jedi facing their fears and doubts, inmates must be willing to face their inner narratives head-on. This confrontation can be facilitated through group dialogue where individuals express what holds them back from achieving their goals. The collective energy of these conversations transforms the group dynamic, showing that vulnerability is not weakness but a strength that fosters healing and growth.

As members witness one another's transformations, they may also gain insights into their own journeys. Observing others succeed or struggle creates powerful learning opportunities. It fosters empathy and encourages reflection on personal progress. This process mirrors the mentorship found in Jedi training, where growth is amplified through positive reinforcement and shared victories.

Forging a path of accountability entails a commitment to self-discipline often the most difficult aspect of personal growth. Jedi training is rigorous, requiring consistency and resilience. Similarly, inmates must challenge themselves daily to remain focused on growth and accountability. Incorporating daily routines can help develop discipline. Simple practices such as meditation, physical exercise, or reading bring structure and foster a disciplined mindset. Consistent engagement with goals imbues individuals with a sense of purpose, motivating them to take ownership of their transformative journeys.

In conjunction with routines and accountability checks, **feedback mechanisms** are also valuable. Structured feedback helps bridge the gap between self-perception and how one's actions are perceived by others. In Jedi training, guidance from mentors is integral to growth. Inmates may find value in asking for feedback from peers in their groups or from facilitators who lead discussions. This process encourages reflection and adaptation based on external insights and can reveal blind spots in self-assessment.

As inmates embark on their journeys of accountability and growth, it is imperative to remain aware of potential setbacks. The path to transformation is not linear; it is often fraught with obstacles. Acknowledging this reality can fortify resolve and inspire persistence. Internal voices of doubt or external pressures may attempt to undermine progress. Jedi teach that remaining steadfast in the face of adversity is essential to reaching one's true potential. Inmates must cultivate resilience and rely on the support of accountability groups to endure moments of difficulty.

To solidify accountability, each individual should engage in a **weekly reflection practice**, assessing progress toward goals. This may involve revisiting journals and vision boards, evaluating strategies that worked and those that did not. Such reflections allow for recalibration of approaches, much like a Jedi reassessing their training regimen. This attention to iterative growth sustains momentum over time and reinforces the concept that accountability is not a one-time effort but a continuous commitment to oneself.

In sum, accountability is a principle that transcends both Jedi teachings and modern psychological practices. Encouraging inmates to take ownership of their journeys nurtures an environment where transformation is possible, rooted in self-improvement and personal responsibility. Through reflection, shared experiences, and a culture of support, inmates can awaken their inner Jedi and embrace the path toward meaningful growth.

As they hold themselves accountable and uplift one another, they will find that the potential for change is not a distant dream but a tangible reality within their grasp. This community of accountability and growth becomes a beacon of hope, illuminating the path ahead. The shared struggles and triumphs stand as a testament to the strength found in unity. Just as Jedi stand shoulder to shoulder in the face of darkness, so too can these individuals find strength among their peers. Through commitment and accountability, they will craft stories not defined by their past but inspired by their capacity for growth a true awakening of the inner Jedi.

Chapter 9: Therapeutic Lightsabers

Integrating Jedi Philosophy with Modern Therapy

As we embark on the journey of weaving together Jedi philosophy with contemporary therapeutic practices, we enter a realm where ancient wisdom meets modern understanding. Jedi teachings, rooted in principles of mindfulness, compassion, and emotional balance, resonate profoundly with many contemporary therapeutic models. This chapter examines various therapeutic models that align harmoniously with Jedi philosophy, outlining how their integration can foster personal growth and facilitate healing particularly in challenging environments such as correctional facilities.

The Jedi Order, renowned for its commitment to peace, understanding, and connection with the Force, provides a unique framework that can enhance therapeutic interventions. The core tenets of Jedi teaching self-awareness, emotional regulation, and altruism parallel the objectives of many therapeutic approaches employed in modern psychology. By merging these philosophies, we can create a comprehensive model that not only addresses mental health issues but also nurtures resilience, purpose, and connection among inmates.

One of the most powerful therapeutic approaches that align with Jedi philosophy is **Cognitive Behavioral Therapy (CBT)**. CBT emphasizes the importance of understanding the connection between thoughts, emotions, and behaviors. Similarly, Jedi teachings advocate for self-reflection and awareness of one's thoughts to cultivate inner peace and clarity. Inmates often grapple with negative thinking patterns that perpetuate cycles of despair and self-defeat. By introducing the cognitive restructuring techniques of CBT within a Jedi framework, therapists can guide individuals to re-evaluate their thoughts and beliefs, fostering a sense of agency and empowerment.

For example, consider the story of **Daniel**, an inmate who struggled with pervasive feelings of worthlessness following a history of trauma. Through CBT, Daniel learned to identify and challenge his negative self-talk. Incorporating Jedi principles, his therapist encouraged him to visualize himself as a Jedi in training, striving to embody the characteristics that made Jedi heroes resilient. This imaginative exercise not only helped Daniel reshape his narrative but also instilled a sense of purpose he was, in a sense, on a path to becoming a better version of himself. The integration of Jedi philosophy provided a motivational framework for Daniel, fueling his commitment to personal growth and healing.

Another approach that parallels Jedi teachings is **Dialectical Behavior Therapy (DBT)**, which emphasizes the balance between acceptance and change. Jedi philosophy promotes a similar duality: understanding that feelings must be acknowledged while also working toward self-improvement. Inmates often face intense emotional turbulence, which can lead to impulsive behaviors or heightened distress. DBT's focus on mindfulness, emotion regulation, and interpersonal effectiveness aligns seamlessly with handling these emotions through a Jedi lens.

For instance, **Sarah**, a young woman incarcerated for her involvement in a gang, found herself in constant emotional upheaval, oscillating between anger and despair. A therapist trained in DBT introduced her to skills for mindfulness, helping her to observe her feelings without judgment. One afternoon, while practicing these skills, her therapist invited her to think of her emotions as part of the Force constantly flowing, sometimes turbulent, yet ultimately manageable. This framing enabled Sarah to distance herself from her emotions, granting her the space to explore healthier responses and interactions with her peers.

In addition to CBT and DBT, **Acceptance and Commitment Therapy (ACT)** offers another intriguing interface between Jedi philosophy and modern therapy. ACT promotes psychological flexibility and encourages individuals to accept their thoughts and feelings while taking committed actions aligned with their values. This approach closely mirrors the Jedi belief in embracing the present moment and understanding one's role in the greater tapestry of existence.

Consider the case of **Tom**, an inmate wrestling with feelings of guilt and shame over his past actions. He felt trapped by his memories, unable to envision a future beyond his sentence. In therapy, Tom learned the ACT principle of *defusion*, a technique that helps individuals separate themselves from their thoughts. His therapist guided him to conceptualize his memories as mere echoes of his past, urging him to view them through the lens of a Jedi who understands the impermanence of all things. By practicing defusion, Tom could step back from his guilt, envisioning himself as a resilient individual capable of growth despite his mistakes.

Furthermore, the use of **mindfulness meditation**, a fundamental aspect of Jedi training, can be effectively integrated into therapeutic practices. Research has consistently shown that mindfulness significantly reduces stress, anxiety, and depression, making it a valuable tool in correctional settings. Jedi meditation, rooted in deep awareness and connection to the Force, mirrors mindfulness practices that encourage inmates to remain present and calm amidst chaos.

Mike, an inmate living with severe anxiety, found solace in mindfulness meditation introduced by his therapist. Initially skeptical, he learned to focus on his breath and center himself, creating a sense of tranquility amid his surroundings. His therapist framed mindfulness as a Jedi technique, where he could harness the Force within him to cultivate calmness and clarity. This connection to Jedi philosophy enhanced Mike's commitment to practice, turning a simple therapeutic exercise into a calling a path toward becoming a "guardian of peace" in his own life.

Beyond individual therapeutic models, **group therapies inspired by Jedi principles** foster communal healing and support among inmates. The process of connecting with others, sharing vulnerabilities, and fostering a sense of belonging echoes the Jedi's commitment to community and collaboration. Group therapy can even utilize role-playing exercises where inmates assume the roles of Jedi, encouraging narratives that emphasize cooperation and mutual aid.

In a successful pilot program, the **"Jedi Council" group therapy initiative** brought together inmates with diverse backgrounds. Using collaborative storytelling, participants shared their experiences while embodying Jedi characters. This collective engagement not only facilitated bonding but also allowed for honest conversations about their struggles. The inmates found strength in their shared narratives, supporting one another while integrating their growth stories into a broader narrative of redemption.

Additionally, incorporating the Jedi concept of **lifelong learning** aligns with the principles of **Positive Psychology**, which emphasize strengths and positive attributes. Positive psychology focuses on fostering well-being and personal development rather than merely addressing mental illness. By emphasizing an inmate's strengths, therapists can guide individuals toward self-discovery and fulfillment, leading to enhanced resilience.

Consider the journey of **Angela**, an inmate identified for her creative talents in art. Her therapist encouraged her to explore her artistic skills as a form of self-expression and healing. Drawing inspiration from Jedi philosophy, the therapist framed Angela's creativity as a unique gift akin to the Force that should be nurtured and developed. This integration not only illuminated Angela's strengths but also ignited a newfound passion within her, ultimately leading to a remarkable transformation.

It is also crucial to acknowledge the role of **storytelling** in both Jedi teachings and therapeutic approaches. The Jedi place great significance on stories, whether they are personal narratives or ancient tales of heroism. Storytelling becomes a transformative tool through which inmates can make sense of their journeys, discover their identities, and envision their futures.

In therapeutic settings, **narrative therapy** can be aligned with Jedi principles to facilitate growth. By helping inmates articulate their stories, therapists encourage them to reclaim their narratives, emphasizing resilience rather than victimization. When inmates share their stories within a supportive environment that respects the Jedi philosophy of compassion and understanding, they can find healing and purpose.

Kyle, a long-term inmate, utilized this approach during an intensive group therapy session. Through the lens of a Jedi, he began to rewrite his narrative, considering the lessons he had learned from his past and the hero he aspired to become. As he learned to articulate his story with empowerment, his peers reflected the same transformation, showing how this integrative approach could create a ripple effect of healing and self-discovery.

As we consider integrating Jedi philosophy with modern therapy, it is paramount to ensure these approaches resonate with the unique experiences and backgrounds of inmates. Acknowledging the complex layers of identity, culture, and trauma is essential to cultivating an environment where Jedi teachings can be embraced and utilized effectively. The implementation of such blended practices requires trained therapists proficient in modern therapeutic modalities and knowledgeable about Jedi philosophies. Ongoing training for mental health professionals should include teachings about the ethical dimensions of Jedi principles, ensuring interventions foster growth, compassion, and ethical action.

In conclusion, the integration of Jedi philosophy with modern therapy has tremendous potential for enhancing the mental health of inmates. Through the principles of self-awareness, emotional regulation, acceptance, and communal connection, therapists can create an environment where individuals thrive even amidst the confines of incarceration. By merging ancient wisdom with contemporary practices, we honor the strength of the human spirit while providing vital tools for rehabilitation and personal growth. The stories of transformation within this framework not only inspire those who participate but also illuminate a path toward healing a reminder that even in our darkest moments, we are never truly alone.

Lightsaber Techniques for Emotional Combat

In the world of Jedi teachings, the lightsaber is not merely a weapon; it is a symbol of responsibility, control, and inner peace. Each movement with the lightsaber embodies not just martial skill but also profound mental resilience and emotional regulation. In applying these teachings to the realm of mental health particularly within the confines of prisons we can find remarkable parallels that allow inmates to engage meaningfully with their emotions and experiences.

This subchapter explores practical techniques that resemble lightsaber practices, promoting self-care and empowerment through mindfulness and visualization elements crucial for emotional combat.

At the core of Jedi training is the concept of **discipline**, a trait that can be wonderfully mirrored in the emotional battles inmates face daily. Much like a Jedi honing their skills, inmates can develop techniques to manage their emotions and interactions through structured practices that cultivate self-awareness and active engagement with their feelings. The combination of mindfulness and action-oriented therapy establishes a foundation for personal empowerment, transformation, and healing.

Mindfulness as the Jedi's First Defense

Mindfulness is a state of active, open attention to the present, where individuals observe their thoughts and feelings without judgment. This mental clarity parallels the focused mind of a Jedi preparing for battle. Just as a Jedi must be aware of their surroundings and their own emotional state, inmates can learn to cultivate mindfulness to better navigate their internal landscapes.

One potent technique involves a simple yet powerful **breathing exercise** that creates calm and control essential tools in both combat and emotional regulation. Begin with the practice of deep breathing, akin to preparing for a lightsaber duel. Inmates can find a quiet space, even within a busy environment, and focus on their breath: inhaling deeply through the nose for a count of four, allowing the chest to expand fully, and exhaling slowly through the mouth for a count of six.

The ebb and flow of breath mirrors the movements of a lightsaber, promoting a rhythm of controlled energy. During this practice, the inmate can visualize themselves wielding a lightsaber, moving with precision and confidence. Each breath becomes a strike against negative emotions, with every exhalation releasing feelings of anger, anxiety, or fear.

As they practice, inmates can reflect on the Jedi principles of patience and perseverance. Each breath represents a moment of stillness before the storm, reinforcing the idea that emotional responses are not instantaneous but can be managed through conscious awareness. This technique reminiscent of the fluidity of lightsaber forms empowers inmates to transform their emotional battlefields into sessions of mindfulness and control. Just as lightsabers defend against external threats, this exercise helps defend against the turmoil of misplaced emotions.

Visualization: Battling Inner Demons

Moving from breathwork into visualizations, inmates can engage their imaginations as Jedi would during training. Visualization serves as a mental rehearsal that prepares individuals for real-life encounters and challenges.

In their minds, inmates can picture themselves as Jedi Knights, equipped with lightsabers, facing challenges that represent their internal struggles be it despair, loneliness, or resentment. In this mental space, they envision themselves wielding their lightsabers with grace and skill, parrying negative thoughts and emotions.

A useful visualization technique involves imagining a specific challenge, such as a difficult interaction with another inmate or the weight of past mistakes. With lightsaber in hand, they confront this challenge head-on. Their opponent becomes a manifestation of personal struggles fear, anger, regret each one more formidable than the last.

The lightsaber symbolizes protection, not only against external dangers but also against internal demons. As they navigate this mental battle, they employ strikes, blocks, and defensive maneuvers that symbolize coping strategies in real life. Every successful strike against negativity reinforces their ability to counter harmful feelings.

Just as Jedi learn from each battle, inmates can reflect on these mental victories, understanding that every moment of control over their emotions is progress. Visualization empowers them to approach reality not as passive participants but as warriors equipped with tools for emotional navigation.

Action-Oriented Practice: Movement as Therapy

Incorporating **action-oriented therapy** encourages inmates to engage not only in their thoughts but also in their physical well-being. Much like a Jedi must maintain physical condition through training, inmates can learn that their bodies and minds are deeply intertwined.

Physical movement especially in group settings can harness the energy of emotional combat for constructive ends. A group session can emulate Jedi training drills, where inmates practice physical fitness alongside emotional exploration. Simulation drills may include striking and blocking motions that mimic lightsaber techniques, allowing inmates to channel emotions through physical expression.

As they move through these drills, they internalize lessons about resilience, teamwork, and shared struggle against internal adversaries. These sessions also emphasize solidarity. Just as Jedi train together, inmates learn that their journeys need not be isolated. Sharing regulation techniques and supporting one another fosters a sense of community and belonging crucial for those who often feel alienated.

Another practice links mindfulness with movement through **martial arts-inspired coping strategies**. Slow-motion sparring, for example, creates a link between body and mind. Each deliberate stance, like the positioning of a lightsaber, affirms a commitment to managing emotions with strength and clarity.

Mindful walking can also strengthen emotional grounding. Inmates take purposeful steps, consciously allowing each foot to connect with the ground while visualizing stability. Every step becomes symbolic of their journey forward, embodying resilience and balance, much like a Jedi standing ready for action.

Reflection and Journaling

To solidify the connection between physical action and emotional regulation, inmates can engage in **journaling** inspired by their practice sessions. After each exercise or emotional engagement activity, they write down observations, feelings, and realizations.

This process serves a dual purpose: articulating emotions while capturing the essence of training, much like a Jedi apprentice logging their journey. Reflections might include lessons learned from imagined lightsaber battles or how physical movements clarified emotions. Such analysis transforms practice into growth.

Through these practical techniques, inmates can cultivate an environment where mental health and emotional resilience are tangible goals akin to mastering a lightsaber. Each meditation, visualization, or mindful motion parallels Jedi training, reinforcing that emotional combat is not a solitary fight but one requiring compassion, support, and connection.

Ultimately, *Lightsaber Techniques for Emotional Combat* demonstrates how Jedi wisdom and modern therapeutic tactics can create a structured environment for self-care and growth. By practicing mindful breathing, visualization, and physically engaging exercises, inmates develop resilience to confront their emotional adversaries.

Through this journey, they learn to wield the metaphorical lightsaber of compassion and strength emerging as empowered individuals ready to walk the path of healing and reconciliation.

Creating a Personal Jedi Plan

In the pursuit of emotional well-being and resilience, the process of self-improvement can often feel daunting, especially within the context of incarceration. However, taking inspiration from the wisdom of the Jedi can empower inmates not only to navigate their circumstances but also to thrive in their personal journeys. This subchapter serves as a guide to constructing a **Personal Jedi Plan**, drawing from the principles of the Force and practical therapeutic techniques. By creating their unique paths toward healing, inmates can harness the energy of the Force to promote inner strength and stability.

The foundation of the Personal Jedi Plan is rooted in **self-awareness and reflection**. By beginning with a deep understanding of their current emotional and mental state, inmates can identify specific areas in need of improvement. It is vital to cultivate an honest and compassionate internal dialogue, encouraging inmates to acknowledge their feelings and experiences without judgment. This step aligns with the Jedi practice of mindfulness, where awareness of the present moment is paramount.

It is recommended that inmates engage in regular self-assessment exercises to reflect on their thoughts, emotions, and behaviors. This can take the form of daily journaling or meditative practices that allow for contemplation and growth.

Defining Personal Goals

Once awareness is established, inmates should define their personal goals, drawing from the lessons of the Jedi. These objectives can be categorized into four domains:

1. **Emotional Regulation**

2. **Relationship Building**

3. **Self-Discipline**

4. **Spiritual Growth**

Each domain offers an opportunity for inmates to explore both their challenges and their aspirations.

- **Emotional Regulation**: Inmates may struggle with anger, anxiety, or sadness. Drawing on Jedi teachings, one approach is to focus on acceptance and letting go, much like Yoda's counsel to embrace emotions without being consumed by them. A practical exercise here could be creating a *feelings wheel*, a visual tool that helps inmates identify and articulate emotions more precisely. By fostering a nuanced understanding of feelings, inmates can respond to emotional states with greater mindfulness and wisdom.

- **Relationship Building**: Even in a structured environment, connections remain vital. The Jedi value collaboration and companionship, recognizing that the Force is amplified through unity. Inmates can cultivate this domain by setting personal goals that prioritize communication, empathy, and trust. One exercise involves role-playing scenarios with peers to practice active listening, building skills in understanding and responding to others' perspectives.

- **Self-Discipline**: A central Jedi principle, discipline can be reinforced through daily routines that promote accountability. Inmates are encouraged to outline a regimen that integrates structured and flexible elements, balancing beneficial habits with time for reflection and relaxation. Morning routines might include physical exercise, meditation, or journaling. Establishing *accountability partners* among peers can further support adherence to these routines, encouraging mutual support and consistency.

- **Spiritual Growth**: This domain invites inmates to explore their values and beliefs meaningfully. Just as Jedi seek a connection with the Force, inmates can benefit from reflecting on their sense of purpose. Guided visualization exercises such as envisioning their ideal selves or post-incarceration lives can help them nurture self-worth and resilience while aligning their actions with long-term aspirations.

Structuring the Plan

121

With goals defined, the **structure of the Personal Jedi Plan** should be created. A standard layout might include:

- Sections for each domain

- Specific goals

- Actionable steps toward each goal

- Methods for tracking progress

Inmates can use a planner, binder, or digital tools (where available) to organize their plans. This structure fosters clarity and allows them to visualize their journey toward emotional and mental well-being.

Accountability and Reflection

Accountability is critical to success. Regular check-ins both individually and with accountability partners reinforce commitment. Weekly or bi-weekly reflections can help inmates assess progress, celebrate successes, and re-evaluate goals when needed. These sessions embody Jedi principles of patience and perseverance.

Setbacks are inevitable. Just as Jedi train continuously and adapt, inmates must recognize that growth is not linear. Including a *learning from setbacks* section in their plan encourages resilience. This practice reminds them that even Jedi face challenges, but they rise again, emboldened by experience.

Integrating Therapeutic Techniques

The final piece of the Personal Jedi Plan is weaving in **therapeutic practices** that enhance emotional and mental health. This may include:

- Mindfulness meditation

- Cognitive behavioral strategies

- Guided imagery

- Creative outlets such as art, writing, or storytelling

Providing a resource list of exercises or activities helps inmates reinforce their progress and strengthens their commitment to growth.

Ultimately, the purpose of a Personal Jedi Plan is to foster **agency and empowerment**. By engaging actively in self-improvement, inmates reclaim control over their lives and destinies. The guiding lights of the Jedi empathy, resilience, self-discipline, and connection illuminate the path to emotional balance and healing.

Implementing such a plan can transform not only individuals but also their communities. Personal growth fosters a more supportive, resilient prison environment where collaboration and understanding thrive.

In conclusion, the journey of self-improvement through Jedi teachings encourages inmates to embrace compassion, pursue emotional healing, and honor their paths toward redemption. By crafting a Personal Jedi Plan, they blend the wisdom of the Force with modern therapeutic practices, creating lives that are balanced, purposeful, and resilient. As they move forward, they carry with them the strength of the Jedi, guiding their actions with integrity and determination.

Chapter 10: Communities of Light

The Power of Community Support

The profound impact of community support in the lives of inmates cannot be overstated. Within the confines of a correctional facility, where isolation can breed despair, the creation of supportive networks becomes an essential lifeline. In the words of Yoda, *"The greatest teacher, failure is,"* but such lessons are often magnified when shared among peers. A community built on Jedi principles not only provides comfort but also fosters an environment conducive to personal growth and transformation. This chapter will delve into the importance of communal support in prison settings through the lens of Jedi teachings, illustrating how shared responsibility can enhance individual development and facilitate rehabilitation.

The journey toward self-discovery and healing is rarely undertaken in solitude. Jedi wisdom emphasizes unity and the strength derived from collaboration. The Force, which binds all living things, is analogous to the connections formed among inmates. These connections can transcend mere friendship; they can evolve into a sisterhood or brotherhood sustained by shared experiences, mutual respect, and trust. In many correctional facilities, inmates often find themselves allied with others who share similar backgrounds or challenges. It is in these relationships that they can exercise the principles of empathy, compassion, and awareness that the Jedi espouse.

Consider the story of a group of inmates at a medium-security prison who decided to create a support circle. Initially, this circle was formed as a response to the heightened tensions of prison life. Inmates began gathering weekly in a vacant room, hoping to find solace in one another's company. At first, the discussions centered on frustrations linked to incarceration lost family connections, the stigma of imprisonment, and the fear of an uncertain future.

However, as they shared their struggles, a deeper sense of camaraderie developed. They began to recognize their individual failures not just as personal setbacks but as collective experiences that could be addressed together.

One member of this group, whom we'll call Lucas, found himself particularly resonating with the Jedi concept of *mindfulness*. As a former gang member, he had accumulated a history of violence and retaliation. Yet, through the support of his peers, Lucas ventured into the realm of vulnerability. He shared his experiences the pain he had inflicted on others, and the regret that lived within him. Inspired by Lucas's courage, others found the strength to share their own stories. In these moments of honesty, they began to practice forgiveness not only of each other but of themselves. Jedi teachings often emphasize the importance of moving beyond past transgressions to embrace a path of healing and growth.

Over time, the support circle transformed from a mere gathering space into a sanctuary where personal breakthroughs flourished. Inmates encouraged one another to pursue educational opportunities, attend therapy sessions, and engage in programs aimed at personal development. This collective responsibility to uplift one another echoed the principles behind the Jedi Order, evoking the idea that *"with great power comes great responsibility."*

Jedi teachings also underscore the importance of mentorship and guidance within communities. In these supportive networks, some inmates have taken on the role of mentors, sharing skills or wisdom with newer members of the group. This sense of mentorship is akin to the Jedi Master–Padawan relationship, where knowledge, skills, and life lessons are passed down, creating a continuous cycle of learning and growth.

In another facility, a program called *Guiding Stars* was initiated, pairing long-term inmates with new arrivals. The veterans, many of whom had undergone significant transformations, volunteered to provide guidance to those just entering the prison system. What began as an effort to acclimate new inmates quickly blossomed into something more profound. The veterans used their own expertise and life lessons many were skilled storytellers to convey the importance of resilience, responsibility, and self-reflection.

Through this program, an unexpected bond formed between the two groups. These mentors inspired their mentees to view incarceration not as an end, but as an opportunity for growth an idea that resonates deeply with Jedi philosophy. They spoke openly about the choices that led them to prison, reinforcing the belief that recognizing one's mistakes has the power to change one's future.

As an example, one mentor, Marcus, had been in and out of the system for over a decade. When he was paired with a young inmate named Jordan, he seized the opportunity to reflect on his own youthful mistakes and regrets. Their relationship flourished, grounded in mutual honesty and trust, as they discussed how fear and anxiety could permeate their lives if not carefully managed. Jordan began to see how he could reshape his narrative, drawing upon the wisdom shared by Marcus. Encouraged by the community, he began participating in educational classes and found solace in artistic expression through writing.

The success of these networks often lies in the shared experiences that bind individuals together. The communal aspect of building support systems cannot be underestimated. They become safe havens where inmates can breathe, reflect, and inspire change. Within this protected space, inmates learn to embrace vulnerability, allowing them to confront their fears and insecurities in a shared setting where they feel empowered to grow.

Furthermore, these communities can serve as a catalyst for accountability. The motivating force of the group can instigate changes in behavior, urging inmates to lean into their personal development. This is reminiscent of how Jedi work in concert, holding each other accountable to the values and tenets of their beliefs.

An illustrative incident occurred during one of the weekly support meetings when a member named Reggie disclosed that he had fallen back into negative patterns something he had vowed to leave behind. Instead of scorn, he was met with understanding and support. One member, Sheila, shared her own bout with relapse. Instead of pushing Reggie away, she pulled him closer, urging him to explore the emotional roots of his struggles. This role of support reflected a core aspect of Jedi teachings: the understanding that everyone falters at times, and that acknowledging those struggles ultimately leads to collective growth.

As the support group continued to thrive, members began organizing community service projects within the prison, reinforcing their bond and altruistic values. Inspired by Jedi principles, inmates sought opportunities to help others, such as creating care packages for those struggling with mental health challenges or organizing educational workshops for fellow inmates. The act of giving back not only strengthened relationships within the group but also served as a reminder of the interconnectedness that Jedi philosophy embraces.

The ripple effects of community support extend far beyond the walls of prison. Inmates who engage in these networks often develop essential social skills that prepare them for successful reintegration into society. The foundations built on shared wisdom, accountability, and support can enable individuals to forge healthier relationships upon release. This fosters a sense of agency and empowerment, reminding those involved that they are capable of change, regardless of their past.

Moreover, the presence of supportive communities fosters a sense of belonging an antidote to the loneliness and isolation often felt within prison walls. Inmates who cultivate relationships that provide emotional and social support experience lower levels of anxiety and depression. This reflects the psychological principle that social support is a critical determinant of mental health, leading to better outcomes for individuals navigating the complex landscape of incarceration.

The Jedi teachings remind us that respect for one another and the bonds we create form the basis of a thriving community. As inmates work to support each other's journeys of self-improvement, they learn to view themselves not solely through the lens of their mistakes, but as members of a collective striving toward shared goals. They begin to understand that their individual growth contributes to the strength of the community a profound realization in the journey of rehabilitation.

In the context of *Communities of Light*, building supportive networks is an essential part of encouraging personal growth. The camaraderie found among inmates serves as a testament to the power of community in fostering resilience and change. As they draw from the wisdom of the Jedi, these individuals cultivate a spirit that is both empowering and uplifting, illuminating paths for healing that might have otherwise remained obscured.

Through shared struggles and triumphs, inmates develop a deeper appreciation for empathy, connection, and mutual support essential elements that define both Jedi teachings and the collective experience of humanity. By fostering communities that embrace these principles, we open the door to transformation and create spaces where hope and healing can flourish.

In conclusion, the journey toward mental well-being and personal growth among inmates is significantly enhanced by the power of community support. The shared responsibility to lift one another mirrors the most profound Jedi teachings, illustrating the transformative impact of connections forged in understanding and empathy. Through tales of resilience and collective responsibility, we see that these bonds do not merely provide comfort; they illuminate pathways toward self-discovery and foster change that can extend far beyond prison walls.

Shared Experiences and Collective Healing

In the dimly lit confines of correctional facilities, where the weight of isolation can feel almost unbearable, the power of shared experiences shines like a beacon of hope. The concept of communities, much like the Jedi Order, is built upon the foundation of unity, understanding, and collective healing. When individuals come together sharing their stories and vulnerabilities they can forge connections that transcend their circumstances. This bond fosters a sense of belonging, nurtures emotional well-being, and encourages personal growth.

Within the framework of a supportive environment, inmates can find solace in their shared narratives. Each person brings a unique story, steeped in struggle, resilience, and dreams unfulfilled. By focusing on these shared experiences, we can cultivate a safe space where empathy flourishes, and the individual becomes part of something greater. The Force, as the Jedi understand it, connects all living things, binding them together in ways that are often unseen. In much the same way, the stories shared among inmates can weave an intricate tapestry of understanding, compassion, and acceptance.

To facilitate this process, structured exercises can be implemented, allowing inmates to share their life stories in a manner that promotes connection and reflection. One effective exercise involves storytelling circles, where participants are encouraged to speak openly about their experiences both the challenges they have faced and the moments that have shaped their identities. This exercise not only enhances communication skills but also cultivates an environment that values each voice. As participants listen to one another, they gain insights into diverse perspectives and situations, fostering empathy and a deeper understanding of the human experience.

Before initiating storytelling circles, it is essential to establish ground rules that honor confidentiality and respect. This foundational step allows participants to feel secure in sharing their narratives without fear of judgment. Facilitators can guide the discussion, reminding everyone of the importance of active listening, maintaining a non-judgmental stance, and offering support to one another. As stories unfold, participants often recognize universal themes of struggle, hope, and growth themes that resonate beyond the walls of confinement.

Another practical exercise designed to deepen these connections is the *Story Exchange.* In this activity, participants pair up and take turns sharing a brief narrative about a pivotal moment in their lives. After each person shares, they provide feedback to their partner, highlighting aspects of the story that they found impactful or relatable. This exchange not only fosters trust and vulnerability but also encourages participants to engage in active listening a skill that is vital for healing and connection.

Jedi philosophy teaches us that every individual is unique yet interconnected by a shared experience of life. Acknowledging this interconnectedness allows participants to reflect on their pathways, recognizing the ways in which they have been shaped not just by their own actions but also by the broader community around them. As stories are exchanged, the barriers that often isolate inmates begin to dissolve. They become each other's mirrors, revealing strengths and weaknesses that they may not have recognized before. By embracing their shared humanity, they can find solace in knowing they are not alone in their struggles.

In addition to storytelling, art can serve as a powerful medium for collective healing. Art therapy exercises that encourage creative expression provide inmates with a non-verbal outlet for their emotions. Drawing, painting, or even collage-making can allow individuals to illustrate their stories without the constraints of language. As they create, participants often uncover layers of their experiences they hadn't previously realized, facilitating deeper emotional connections with themselves and others.

Group art projects can further enhance the sense of community. Inmates can collaborate on murals or other large-scale art pieces, working together toward a common goal. This not only fosters a feeling of teamwork but also instills a sense of pride and ownership in their shared environment. Each brushstroke, each color choice, and each creative decision is a testament to their collective journey, embodying the spirit of healing and unity.

Moreover, dialogue around mindfulness can complement these exercises. Invoking practices that foster presence and awareness allows participants to connect with their emotions more profoundly. Mindfulness techniques, such as guided meditations, can help inmates become attuned to their thoughts and feelings, facilitating a deeper understanding of their personal stories and the stories of those around them. Encouraging them to be present while sharing their experiences acknowledging both the beauty and pain of their narrative creates an environment conducive to collective healing.

As inmates share their stories, they may also engage in thematic discussions that highlight the broader societal issues contributing to their circumstances. Exploring themes such as addiction, trauma, and resilience can open up dialogues that empower participants. Rather than seeing their experiences solely through the lens of victimhood, they can embrace a narrative of survival and growth. This reframing is pivotal for mental health; it enables inmates to reclaim their identities, weaving resilience into their individual and collective stories.

Facilitators can enhance these discussions by integrating teachings from the Jedi Code that emphasize compassion, understanding, and the interconnectedness of all beings. For instance, exploring the tenet of compassion and how it applies not just to themselves but to their families, friends, and communities can help deepen participants' empathy for one another. This allows for the cultivation of a supportive network, one where individuals feel uplifted and recognized, fostering a loving environment where healing can truly take place.

To further instill a sense of belonging, the practice of creating *community affirmations* can be introduced. Inmates can collaborate to identify positive affirmations that resonate with the group's shared values, hopes, and aspirations. These affirmations can be written, illustrated, and displayed prominently within their shared space as a daily reminder of their commitment to one another and their ongoing journeys of healing. This visual representation of their collective strength can reinforce their sense of unity, reminding each participant that they are part of something meaningful.

In the spirit of fostering ongoing connection, regular follow-up sessions can also be established. This consistency helps to maintain the bonds formed during initial exercises while encouraging continued storytelling and dialogue. During these sessions, participants can share their progress, reflect on lessons learned, and celebrate each other's successes, however small. This longitudinal approach to community building mirrors the Jedi belief in the power of enduring relationships. It acknowledges that healing and growth are ongoing processes that thrive in the context of supportive networks.

As inmates delve into shared experiences, they not only work through their individual challenges but also nurture a collective resilience based on compassion and understanding. The act of sharing of being vulnerable can transform lives, providing a sense of agency that may have been lost during confinement. Through the embodiment of Jedi principles, inmates are not just participants in a program; they become a community bound by their shared commitment to growth and healing.

Throughout these processes, it is crucial to be mindful of the physical and emotional safety of all participants. Facilitators must remain attentive, ensuring that everyone feels heard and respected. As stories can evoke strong emotions, creating a supportive ambiance where individuals can process their feelings in real time is essential. Checking in with participants regularly, allowing for breaks or elements of self-care during intense sharing sessions, and being open to exploring deeper emotional issues that arise are all integral parts of maintaining a safe space for sharing.

Ultimately, the concept of shared experiences within prisons has the power to ignite the light within each individual. By embracing the emotional healing that occurs through storytelling, art, mindfulness, and connection, inmates can begin to transform their narratives. Each story shared becomes a step toward healing an assertion of identity, resilience, and the acknowledgment of one's place within a community.

As these individuals begin to see themselves reflected in one another, the realization that they are not isolated becomes increasingly clear. They are not alone. The Jedi's teachings on the interconnectedness of all things can guide them to understand that their stories contribute to a larger narrative of hope, empathy, and healing. In this union, they find the strength to confront their pasts while envisioning brighter futures.

By believing in the efficacy of shared experiences, correctional facilities can become breeding grounds for collective healing a true manifestation of *Communities of Light.* As inmates embrace their stories and connect through universal experiences, they breed hope, compassion, and resilience, fostering an environment where each individual can reclaim their narrative and contribute to the healing of others. They become not just students of the Force but agents of change, illuminating the path for both themselves and their fellow community members. In healing one another, they cultivate a lasting legacy of light amidst the shadows of their confinement.

Creating Light Together

By drawing on the wisdom of the Jedi and combining it with modern practices from mental health care, we can help inmates establish vital connections with one another. Through shared experiences and insights, they can illuminate their paths to recovery and transformation.

Imagine a small room within the prison walls, filled with the low hum of chatter as inmates gather for a workshop designed not just for learning, but for nurturing human connections. Each person arrives with a story, a background of trials and triumphs, and the unyielding desire to find purpose amidst the confines of their environment. They carry their burdens into this space, but instead of feeling the weight of isolation, they are greeted by an atmosphere of acceptance a sense of belonging reminiscent of the Jedi Council itself, where diverse voices come together for the common good.

The workshop begins with a simple yet powerful exercise: sharing personal strengths. As the facilitator invites each person to reflect on a quality they value in themselves, the room fills with affirmations. *"I am resilient." "I am compassionate." "I am creative."* These words resonate, bouncing off the walls and transforming them into a sanctuary of light. In this act, individuals awaken their inner Jedi, realizing that their qualities can act as beacons of hope not just for themselves, but for others around them.

This kind of communal activity can serve multiple purposes. It acts as a platform for building self-esteem, enhancing interpersonal skills, and creating a network of support. The inmates who participate in these workshops often report feeling a sense of empowerment that transcends their immediate circumstances. They learn to listen and to share in vulnerability, fusing their energies to generate a powerful force of solidarity. This communal bond, much like the connection that extends among Jedi, becomes a source of strength as they face daily challenges.

Consider the story of Marcus, a 32-year-old inmate who once struggled deeply with feelings of worthlessness. He participated in one such workshop, initially resistant to the power of sharing and community. On the final day, when he was invited to articulate the changes he felt during these sessions, he stood up, hesitated, but then grasped the courage to speak. *"I never thought I could be someone others might look up to,"* he said, his voice steady. *"But these workshops taught me that by sharing my struggles, I can help others, too."* The room erupted in applause, each clap echoing with affirmation and respect.

But these initiatives don't only encompass workshops. Support groups are invaluable in creating spaces where inmates can discuss specific challenges addiction, trauma, family dynamics within a nurturing environment. Here, the principles of empathy, understanding, and shared experience guide discussions. Participants come to realize that their struggles, however isolating they may feel, are shared by many. Combining the teachings of Jedi philosophy, which emphasize compassion and awareness, with therapeutic techniques enables a deeper connection to both self and community.

Take the example of a support group that focuses on grief and loss, led by trained counselors and supported by inmate facilitators. In these sessions, members recount the profound losses that have affected them whether through the death of loved ones, the loss of dreams due to incarceration, or the heartbreak of estrangement from families. This environment allows collective mourning, validating the emotions that often lie buried beneath layers of shame and guilt.

During one session, a young inmate named Elena spoke candidly about losing her brother. Her story caused ripples of empathetic nods around the circle, compelling others to share similar losses. As they spoke, the discussion moved into the realm of memory how they honor their loved ones and navigate the pain of absence. Discussions turned toward what it means to create new legacies even in the face of adversity. They learned from one another about coping mechanisms, healthy expressions of grief, and the importance of holding space for each other's stories.

Creating support groups fosters a culture of accountability, where inmates hold one another to healthy behaviors much like Jedi supporting each other in their paths toward enlightenment and mastery. They become a unit working toward a common goal: emotional regulation, healing, and personal growth. With the guiding wisdom of shared experiences, they empower each other to seek first understanding and then forgiveness, helping to transform individual burdens into communal strength.

Learning circles serve another critical function in this journey of collective growth. These circles can focus on personal development, discussing topics such as anger management, mindfulness, conflict resolution, and emotional intelligence. The circles are open forums, where inmates feel free to express their thoughts and questions without judgment. The format promotes brainstorming and values each participant's perspective, creating a tapestry of diverse ideas and strategies.

One learning circle, themed around *"The Force of Forgiveness,"* became instrumental for many. Utilizing a combination of Jedi teachings especially the acknowledgment that holding onto anger only serves to imprison the self and therapeutic principles of restorative justice, participants were invited to reflect on personal grievances and explore the concept of releasing resentment. Through guided practices, such as writing letters to those they felt wronged by, even if those letters never reached their intended recipients, the inmates liberated themselves from emotional chains.

Carlos, a self-proclaimed cynic when he entered the learning circle, found himself deeply moved by the discussions surrounding forgiveness. Initially, he viewed it as a weakness, believing that to forgive was somehow to overlook his pain. But through sharing and listening, he began to understand the Jedi philosophy that forgiveness is not condoning it is freeing oneself from the continuous cycle of pain. He shared his letter during a reading session, expressing his thoughts and ultimately seeking closure. The wave of emotional vulnerability in the room provided Carlos with a new lens through which to view his relationships and grievances.

As these initiatives take root, the positive changes ripple throughout the community. Those who engage in workshops, support groups, and learning circles become ambassadors of light; they carry their insights back to their peers, sparking ripples of change that extend far beyond the confines of their gatherings. The synergy creates a recognized culture of support and growth, slowly transforming the prison into a sanctuary of healing, respect, and mutual empowerment.

The sense of responsibility that arises from these activities is profound. Inmates start to realize that their actions, attitudes, and expressions of empathy can guide not only their own journeys but also have the potential to affect others. The collective effort exemplifies the principle of unity within the Jedi ethos that the Force connects all living things, and together, they can harness that power to uplift one another.

Such community-driven efforts are not simple undertakings; they require vision, enthusiasm, and resilience. Creating these programs may start small, even with just a handful of willing participants, but with time and commitment, they can expand into comprehensive networks that redefine the prison culture. The transformational journey encompasses difficulties and setbacks, but the same resolve and support systems that help individuals face their struggles can fortify these initiatives.

For prison staff and mental health professionals engaging in these programs, it is crucial to empower inmates to take leadership roles within workshops and circles. Trusting inmates with responsibility cultivates a deeper sense of ownership and pride. It aligns with the Jedi notion of instilling confidence and encouraging mentorship guiding others while simultaneously learning oneself.

Consider the example of Inmate Counselor James, who once participated in a workshop and later felt compelled to facilitate. Initially apprehensive, he employed the skills he learned to create a welcoming space where new participants felt safe. James's transformation from participant to facilitator exemplifies the core Jedi belief: once you learn, you must teach. By passing on his knowledge, he amplified the circle's power and influence. His experience mirrored many other inmates, each of whom could conquer their own self-doubt while uplifting their community in the process.

As we conclude this subchapter, the vision of *creating light together* shines brightly. It resonates with the Jedi tenet of mutual respect, support, and the unwavering commitment to the greater good. Building initiatives in prisons through workshops, support groups, and learning circles strengthens community spirit and paves the way for personal transformation. These endeavors foster an environment where individuals can confront their challenges, articulate their fears, and inspire one another toward healing.

The journey toward collective empowerment may never fully culminate, yet it thrives through the steadfast engagement of those willing to share, listen, and participate. A legacy of shared learning emerges, guiding each member of the community much like the guiding hand of a mentor to a young Jedi illuminated by hope, healing, and the promise of brighter horizons.

In opening ourselves to the possibilities of connection and support, we discover not only the light within ourselves but also the potential to ignite that light in others. Together, we can create a force for good: a vibrant community that encourages every individual to rise from the shadows and step into their most authentic selves.

Chapter 11: From Suffering to Strength

Reflecting on Transformation

In the dim light of a small prison cell, surrounded by bare walls and the muffled sounds of life beyond, a man named David found himself in a moment of profound reflection. He had once been consumed by a cycle of anger, addiction, and despair, but after years of battling his demons, he was beginning to sense a change within himself, akin to a flickering light in the far reaches of a darkened room.

David's journey was not just a tale of survival but a testament to the power of transformation a story woven with the wisdom of Jedi philosophy and the comforting embrace of modern therapeutic practices, resonating with a healing force.

Like many others in his predicament, David's descent into chaos began during a period of immense pressure and a desperate need to escape the weight of reality. He had turned to substance abuse, seeking solace in the numbing effects of drugs. His life quickly spiraled out of control, leading him down a path that resulted in his imprisonment. However, it was in this very space meant for punishment that he discovered the potential for rebirth.

It was one afternoon during a group therapy session that a pivotal moment occurred. The facilitator introduced a unique framework for processing one's past a blend of cognitive behavioral techniques and Jedi teachings. *"You are not just your failures,"* the facilitator said, echoing the wisdom of Jedi Master Yoda's words: *"The greatest teacher, failure is."*

In that moment, David realized that he was not defined by his mistakes but could instead harness them as steppingstones toward growth.

As the sessions progressed, David began to internalize the concept of transformation. He listened to the stories of fellow inmates, each narrative filled with pain but also the seeds of resilience. There was Michael, who had lost his brother to violence and sought redemption through art, pouring his heart onto canvases. Maria, who had battled severe depression, shared how connecting to her spirituality through meditation helped her reclaim her sense of self.

These were more than stories; they were manifestations of the inner light each individual possessed, waiting to be ignited.

In crafting his own narrative, David reflected on a particularly challenging moment the day he was arrested. At that instant, despair had threatened to blanket him entirely, yet now he recognized it as a catalyst for change. The ripple effects of his actions had devastated not only himself but his family as well.

In this acknowledgment lay the first step of transformation: acceptance.

His emotional release gradually morphed despair into determination. He began to see his incarceration as an opportunity, a chance to rebuild his life on firmer foundations. Within the confines of the prison walls, while the outside world continued unabated, David took to practices that connected him to the essence of the Force. He embraced mindfulness meditation, learning to center himself amidst turmoil.

The process was not instantaneous, and there were days when anxiety clawed at his insides. Yet with each practice, he felt a semblance of calm wash over him, echoing the tranquility that Jedi Knights sought in moments of chaos. This connection to breath, to presence, grounded him in ways he had never experienced before. It became a source of strength, enabling him to face the ghosts of his past with grace rather than fear.

Transformation is often misunderstood as a linear progression, but it is much more akin to a dance two steps forward, one step back. David experienced this rhythm vividly. There were setbacks; he faced moments of doubt and temptation, particularly during the holidays when the absence of family became a glaring reminder of what he had lost.

In these moments of vulnerability, he would recall the teachings of the Jedi about embracing one's feelings without judgment. He understood that grief and yearning were as valid as hope and joy, and it was through this acceptance that a new strength emerged.

Each day, David actively challenged himself to engage with his feelings rather than suppress them. He began to journal, confronting both the darkness and light within his soul. In those pages, he penned not just his fears and regrets but also his dreams and aspirations, often imagining a future enriched by the lessons he was learning. Much like a Jedi preparing for battle, he equipped himself with self-awareness, mindfulness, and a commitment to becoming a better version of himself.

This act of self-reflection illuminated another truth: transformation is not a solitary journey. It intertwines with the lives of others, creating an intricate web of shared experiences. David found solace in the connections he formed with fellow inmates. They became a support system a community bound by the desire for change. In their shared moments, stories emerged, each a unique testimony to the strength that can arise from suffering.

The laughter, the tears, the encouragement passed among them became catalysts for a collective transformation that reverberated through the prison walls.

The significance of vulnerability became evident to David, mirroring the teachings of the Jedi. Authentic strength is not an absence of fear but a brave engagement with it. In sharing his own road from darkness to light, he inspired others to discover their paths to transformation. They discussed their struggles openly in the safe space fostered by the therapeutic sessions, each word like a lightsaber a tool to carve through the shadows.

It became clear that suffering could lead to profound insights and strengths that no one had anticipated when they first stepped into confinement.

As the months turned into years, David transformed his understanding of freedom. He once equated it strictly with physical release from prison, but he learned that true freedom arises from within. It was the freedom to choose how he responded to his circumstances, the empowerment to reshape his identity, and the decision to define himself not by past mistakes, but by the strength he had cultivated through them.

With every new insight, he felt more like a Jedi in training, learning the ways of the Force and navigating the complexities of life with wisdom and compassion.

Through yoga and physical exercise, David began to cultivate another form of strength: resilience of the body. A small group formed, where inmates met daily to practice yoga. The physical challenge of stretching and balancing felt liberating; with each session, he forged a connection between body and spirit, cultivated through discipline and mindfulness. Every deep breath on the mat echoed the teachings of the Jedi, where physical mastery was as crucial as mental fortitude.

This harmonization of body and mind became a tribute to what it meant to truly transform.

In the broader context, David understood that transformation is often resisted by societal stigmas. The world outside still tended to view inmates as irredeemable, lost to their transgressions. Yet David had tasted the truth of redemption firsthand. He envisioned a future where he could advocate for others, sharing his story not as a point of shame but as a beacon of hope. The Jedi philosophy of service to others the notion that true strength lies in uplifting those around you became a guiding principle.

As his release date approached, David felt a blend of excitement and apprehension swirl within him. He had spent nearly a decade laying the groundwork for his new life, honing the skills and wisdom cultivated in the dark. He was not stepping into the world as the man who had entered prison but as someone transformed an embodiment of the struggle and beauty of rebirth.

He began to prepare for this next chapter by mapping out goals, envisioning a life rooted in service and advocacy, sharing Jedi wisdom interwoven with modern therapeutic understandings to help others heal.

On the day of his release, the air outside tasted different, vibrant and alive. As David stepped through the gates of the prison, a rush of conflicting emotions enveloped him fear of the unknown, elation at newfound freedom, and gratitude for the journey he had undertaken. Yet a newfound strength surged within him, reminding him of the lessons learned and the promise he made to himself.

The years spent in incarceration had not just altered his trajectory; they had catalyzed a metamorphosis of heart and mind. He saw the world through a lens of compassion and understanding, recognizing that every individual possesses the power to transcend their struggles much like the path of a Jedi, marked by trials but equally filled with the possibilities of light.

As David ventured forth into a new dawn, he understood that the journey of transformation is continuous. The struggles he faced would remain a part of him, but they would no longer anchor him down they would serve as wings, propelling him toward his life's purpose. He was ready to embrace this ongoing evolution and illuminate the path for others seeking strength in their suffering.

In summation, the essence of transformation resides not in the absence of struggle, but in the journey through it. It is a testament to the resilience of the human spirit, a narrative of reclaiming agency, refined through adversity. Just as the Jedi teach that hope can emerge from despair, so too can individuals facing their shadows find strength.

David's story, emblematic of this journey, is a beacon of possibility an invitation to embrace our narratives as we strive from suffering to strength, and from darkness into light. Ultimately, transformation is to acknowledge our experiences fully, to stand steadfast in our truth, and to hope. And in this pursuit lies the great, enduring power within us all.

A Future of Possibilities

The journey through incarceration can often feel like an endless cycle of loss, despair, and disillusionment. However, it is vital to understand that suffering can be transformed into strength, paving the way toward a future filled with possibilities. In the face of daunting challenges, every inmate has the opportunity to rise, embrace their inner strength, and visualize a life that goes beyond the confines of their current circumstances.

To aid in this transformation, it is essential to reflect on personal experiences, recognize the lessons learned, and utilize Jedi teachings to instill hope and courage. Embracing the Force means tapping into an inner reservoir of power one that can illuminate the path ahead and serve as a guide through uncertainty. This subchapter serves as a beacon, laying out clear pathways for realizing a brighter future, encouraging inmates to envision their dreams, and presenting practical steps for achieving them.

A critical first step in manifesting a future of possibilities is **self-reflection**. In the quiet moments of solitude, take the time to assess your journey thus far. What experiences have shaped you? What lessons have emerged from the struggles faced? Like a Jedi who meditates on their past, examining both triumphs and failures can provide invaluable insights and foster growth.

Journaling can be an effective tool during this process. Put pen to paper to articulate thoughts, feelings, and aspirations. This practice can clarify the mind and chart the course toward healing. It is also crucial to connect feelings of suffering with newfound strength. Each daunting moment can become a catalyst for personal evolution if framed correctly. Reflect on past pain and consider how it has contributed to your resilience. Jedi teachings emphasize mindfulness and presence, encouraging individuals to understand their emotions without being defined by them. Harnessing this Jedi approach allows for the recognition of challenges as opportunities for growth. Instead of viewing suffering as an endpoint, see it as a beginning an invitation to evolve into a stronger version of yourself.

Once you have acknowledged the strength born from suffering, the next step is to **visualize a future filled with possibilities**. Imagine a life beyond the prison walls. What does it look like? What dreams and ambitions do you have? Picture them in vivid detail. A Jedi often uses visualization techniques to align their thoughts with their intentions, creating a spiritual blueprint for success. The clearer the picture you paint in your mind, the more attainable those dreams can become.

Visualization is a powerful tool that can enhance motivation and inspire action. Take time to create a vision board a collage of images, words, and symbols that represent your aspirations. Place it in a location where you will see it daily as a reminder of what you are working toward. This visual representation serves to focus your energy on your goals and maintain momentum throughout the journey ahead.

In addition to visualization, it is essential to **set achievable personal goals**. Break down your aspirations into actionable steps, making them bite-sized to prevent feelings of overwhelm. Consider the SMART criteria for goal setting: Specific, Measurable, Achievable, Relevant, and Time-bound. For example, if your vision includes pursuing education, set a specific goal of completing a certain number of courses within a delineated timeframe. This approach provides clarity and creates milestones to celebrate along the way, maintaining motivation as you progress.

As you work toward these goals, seek **support from others**. Embrace the concept of community a cornerstone of Jedi philosophy. Isolation can breed despair, while connection fosters hope. Engage with fellow inmates who share similar aspirations or interests. Support each other in overcoming obstacles and celebrate achievements together. By creating a network of encouragement, you can uplift those around you while reinforcing your own strength and resolve.

In the spirit of a Jedi, pay attention to the power of **positive affirmations**. Speak kindly to yourself; remind yourself of your worth and capabilities. Negative self-talk can be incredibly damaging, leading to feelings of inadequacy and hopelessness. Instead, harness the Force within to affirm your potential. Create a set of personalized affirmations that resonate with you, such as *"I am capable of achieving my dreams"* or *"My past does not define my future."* Reciting these affirmations each day can instill a sense of purpose and facilitate a more positive outlook.

It is also essential to cultivate a **mindset of gratitude**. Amid struggles and hardships, look for reasons to be thankful. This practice aligns with the Jedi path, which emphasizes balance and awareness of the present moment. Take time each day to reflect on three things for which you are grateful. This can transform your perspective and highlight the beauty that often gets overshadowed by challenges. Gratitude allows you to appreciate the journey, reinforcing the connection to your inner strength.

Forgiveness is another powerful element in the pursuit of a brighter future. Just as Jedi are taught to let go of anger and resentment, you too can benefit from releasing the weight of past grievances. Holding onto grudges can hinder personal growth and restrict your ability to move forward. Consider the people, experiences, or even aspects of yourself that require forgiveness. This process may take time, but finding the courage to forgive can free you from the chains of the past and open you to healing and new possibilities.

The road to recovery and reinvention is not always linear. Challenges and setbacks may arise, but it is critical to view them as part of the journey rather than as insurmountable obstacles. Acknowledge the feelings that come with these moments of struggle, but do not allow them to dictate your will or determination. Reflecting on the Jedi mantra *"Failure is an opportunity to learn"* allows you to approach difficulties with a mindset geared toward growth. Resilience is built through perseverance; each time you rise after a fall, you strengthen your ability to overcome future challenges.

As you progress on your path, consider incorporating **mindfulness practices** that align with the principles of the Force. Meditation and deep breathing can ground you, helping to manage stress and anxiety. By learning to calm your mind and center your thoughts, you can enhance your focus on achieving goals and envisioning your future. The practice of being present in the moment is a powerful antidote to worries about what lies ahead.

Utilizing the power of the Force further involves exploring your **passions and interests**. Engage in activities that inspire and ignite creativity. Whether it is drawing, writing, or practicing a new skill, expressing yourself is an integral component of personal growth.

This exploration not only provides a release but can help you uncover potential career paths or hobbies that you can pursue once you leave the confines of incarceration.

Education serves as a crucial resource in crafting a future of possibilities. Take full advantage of any educational programs available within the facility. Learning new skills can enhance your sense of self-worth and provide you with the tools needed to thrive post-incarceration. Consider exploring vocational training programs that may lead to stable employment in fields that pique your interest. This proactive approach echoes the Jedi commitment to knowledge and preparedness.

As the chapter of your life within incarceration begins to shift toward one of purpose and empowerment, remember the importance of **resilience in adapting to new environments**. Life can be unpredictable, much like navigating the trials of a Jedi. However, embracing flexibility and adaptability can position you to seize opportunities that arise unexpectedly. Develop a mindset that welcomes change and sees it as an avenue for growth rather than a hindrance.

Reflect on this journey from suffering to strength; each experience along the way informs the person you aspire to become. The future you envision is not merely a figment of hope; it is a tangible reality waiting to be crafted. The Force resides within you, guiding your decisions and illuminating your path toward personal fulfillment.

In conclusion, the future is a vast expanse of possibilities, and each inmate has the power to shape their own destiny. By embracing reflection, setting actionable goals, strengthening relationships, nurturing a positive mindset, and committing to education and skill development, hope can flourish even in the most challenging environments.

As you cultivate the Jedi wisdom learned throughout this book, know that the journey from suffering to strength is not meant to be traveled alone. You have the capacity to inspire those around you, becoming a source of light in a world that often feels shadowed by adversity.

In the face of challenges, remember that every obstacle is an opportunity waiting to be claimed. Embrace the journey ahead as you navigate the path toward healing, growth, and a life illuminated by the possibilities that lie beyond these walls. Your future holds the promise of greatness believe in that truth, harness the power of the Force within, and step boldly into the reality you have the power to create.

Final Thoughts and Call to Action

In the tapestry of life, each of us weaves a unique story, marked by challenges, triumphs, and the pursuit of purpose. In the context of prison, where the shadows often loom larger than the light, it becomes essential to remember that behind every uniform, behind every steel door, and behind every guarded moment, there exists a spirit yearning for connection, understanding, and redemption.

As we conclude this exploration of how Jedi wisdom and modern medicine can illuminate the path from suffering to strength, it is vital to recognize the narratives we all share in the pursuit of mental well-being. Throughout this journey, we have traversed the realms of emotional resilience, empathy, and hope. We have learned that just as the Jedi embrace the Force, individuals grappling with inner struggles can also tap into a deeper source of strength.

The challenges faced within prison from isolation and despair to trauma and regret can feel insurmountable. Yet the teachings drawn from Jedi philosophy remind us that even in the darkest moments, the light of hope can shine brightly. In drawing upon this wisdom, we understand that resilience is more than mere endurance; it is an active practice of confronting challenges and transforming them into paths for growth.

This final section serves as a call to action, urging each reader to continue engaging with the transformative concepts we have explored. The principles of resilience, empathy, and hope extend beyond these pages. They demand application in our daily lives and interactions, guiding decisions and fostering meaningful connections.

Resilience

Resilience calls on us to confront challenges head-on, using past experiences to inform our present responses. Our collective stories woven with struggles and victories remind us that growth is not linear. It is a process adorned with both setbacks and triumphs. By embracing our own battles, we create a ripple effect, instilling hope in those who may feel trapped by their circumstances. As we uplift ourselves through narratives of strength, we help others discover their own potential for change.

Empathy

Empathy is perhaps the most vital tool for re-establishing connections, particularly among those who have felt marginalized. Jedi teachings encourage us to perceive beyond the surface, to seek understanding, to listen, and to validate the experiences of others. This humanity binds us together.

By fostering empathy, we break down the barriers that isolating environments like prisons often erect. It becomes imperative that we enact empathy in daily life reaching out to those in our communities who may be struggling, including inmates, their families, or peers facing unseen battles. Empathy is a potent force, reminding us that we are never alone in our struggles.

Hope

Hope is the beacon that guides us through the darkest tunnels. While the world, especially within prison, can sometimes feel bleak, it is vital to remember that hope exists even in the smallest actions: a smile, a kind word, or a moment of understanding. By cultivating hope within ourselves and others, we create an environment that fosters growth and healing.

Invite hope into your interactions. Provide encouragement. Inspire those around you to seek their light, even when it feels distant. A simple reminder that a person's story is not over can revive the spirit.

A Call to Action

As we navigate our paths beyond these pages, let us rekindle our commitment to embody resilience, empathy, and hope not as abstract ideals, but as actionable commitments. Volunteer. Mentor. Support communities that aid inmates. Encourage those inside to explore unseen possibilities by offering mentorship, resources, and validation. Facilitate conversations that normalize their experiences while amplifying their efforts toward recovery.

Engagement with mental health is not just individual; it is also collective. Advocate for systemic change. Work toward creating cnvironments both within and outside prison walls that support mental well-being. Push for policies that address mental health needs, expand educational programs, and promote rehabilitation. By joining forces with mental health professionals, community organizations, and policymakers, we can help transform the landscape of care for inmates, ensuring access to the resources necessary for healing and growth.

Sharing Jedi wisdom and principles of mental well-being is a noble path. Reflect on your own experiences and consider how you can radiate these teachings into your surroundings. Create spaces where others feel safe to express their vulnerabilities and seek assistance. Through shared openness, we can dismantle the structures of shame and isolation that pervade our society.

Carrying the Light Forward

Let us not forget the stories of hope that emerge when these principles are lived. For every individual who once faced despair, countless others have transformed their journeys, finding strength through connection and support. Share these stories freely. Uplift others with tangible accounts of resilience. Encourage those in despair to envision their potential for change and guide them toward healing.

Above all, hold fast to the truth that our stories are ongoing. The journey from suffering to strength is not a destination but a continuous evolution. Every setback paves the way for a comeback. Every victory, no matter how small, deserves to be celebrated. Within inmate communities and beyond, reinforce this belief using Jedi wisdom as a guiding light for redemption and growth.

With these final thoughts, we embrace the spirit of the Jedi in acknowledging that even from the darkest trials, we can become warriors of hope, advocates of change, and torchbearers of resilience. This journey continues with the understanding that every action, no matter how small, contributes to light in a world often fraught with shadows.

Your commitment to resilience, empathy, and hope will not only shape your individual path but also spark a movement of healing, understanding, and renewed strength.

Closing Reflection

Embark on this mission with courage, for every moment offers an opportunity for growth. Cultivate resilience. Radiate empathy. Share hope as guiding principles in your life. The future is not predetermined; it is crafted through each choice and action taken today.

Together, let us move beyond the pages of this book into a world where the power of our stories heals, uplifts, and transforms lives. Together, as compassionate warriors of the light, we can extend the reach of the Force, illuminating the way for those caught in darkness and guiding them toward their own journeys of strength and redemption.

Chapter 12: The Adventure Continues

And here we are, at the end of our journey together! What an incredible ride this has been. I'm filled with gratitude that you decided to take this leap with me. Thank you for lending me your eyes and minds, for diving deep into these pages filled with dreams, challenges, and triumphs. Your presence means the world to me, and I hope you've enjoyed every moment as much as I enjoyed creating it.

As we close this book, I encourage you to pause and reflect on what you've encountered. Did a character or situation resonate with you? I hope that amidst the chaos and joy of this collection, you discovered pieces of yourself. Often, it's the unexpected elements that leave the deepest impact, and my greatest hope is that you'll carry these stories with you long after the final page.

But let's not stop here! This book may be closing, but the adventure doesn't end we're simply reloading our imaginations for the next quest. I urge you to take these narratives into the world: share them, explore your own stories, and dive into new ones. Read widely. Let every word inspire you to create your own magic.

Stories echo within us, and I hope these have sparked the creativity you hold inside. Scribble down your own tales, let your imagination run free, and remember you have the power to weave ideas into existence, just as I did. Now it's your turn to contribute to the cycle of creativity that connects us all.

I'm beyond excited to hear how these stories may have influenced you, or how they might awaken new thoughts and insights. Your journey has only just begun keep exploring, keep questioning, and keep imagining. Let's make this a dialogue, not a monologue. I can't wait to connect with you and hear your reflections as we continue onward in our adventures.

So, thank you from the bottom of my adventurous heart! May the stories you discover and create illuminate your path. Remember, we're all in this together, navigating the wild seas of storytelling and inspiration. Keep believing in the magic of words, and see where they take you next.

Until we meet again, may your adventures be bold and your nights filled with wondrous tales. Here's to the next chapter of this amazing journey we call life!

With endless gratitude,

Richard R. Dudley

www.ingramcontent.com/pod-product-compliance
Lightning Source LLC
Chambersburg PA
CBHW061803120626
46550CB00005B/2111